Calendar

S0-CCY-735

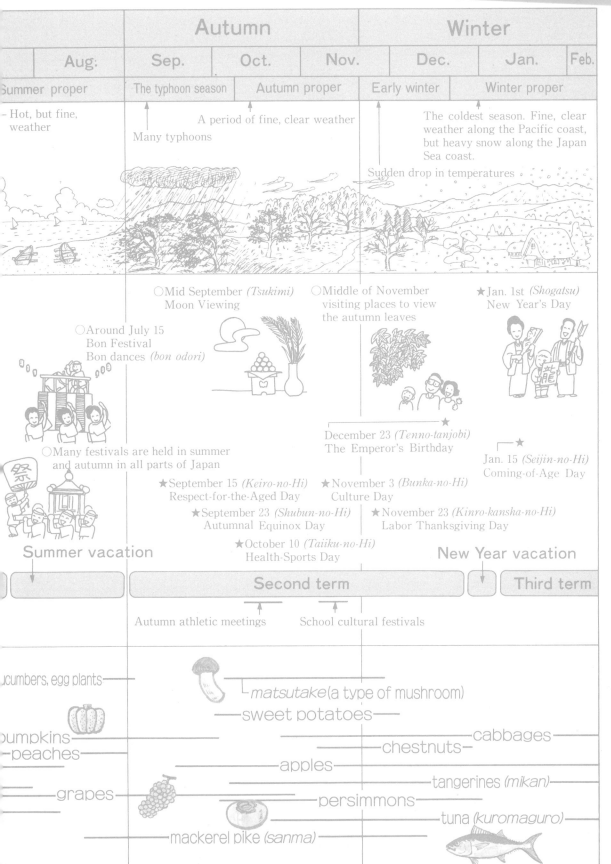

		Autumn			Winter		
	Aug.	Sep.	Oct.	Nov.	Dec.	Jan.	Feb.
Summer proper		The typhoon season	Autumn proper		Early winter	Winter proper	

– Hot, but fine, weather

A period of fine, clear weather

Many typhoons

The coldest season. Fine, clear weather along the Pacific coast, but heavy snow along the Japan Sea coast.

Sudden drop in temperatures

○Mid September *(Tsukimi)*
Moon Viewing

○Middle of November
visiting places to view the autumn leaves

★Jan. 1st *(Shogatsu)*
New Year's Day

○Around July 15
Bon Festival
Bon dances *(bon odori)*

December 23 *(Tenno-tanjobi)*
The Emperor's Birthday

○Many festivals are held in summer and autumn in all parts of Japan

★ ──
Jan. 15 *(Seijin-no-Hi)*
Coming-of-Age Day

★September 15 *(Keiro-no-Hi)*
Respect-for-the-Aged Day

★November 3 *(Bunka-no-Hi)*
Culture Day

★September 23 *(Shubun-no-Hi)*
Autumnal Equinox Day

★November 23 *(Kinro-kansha-no-Hi)*
Labor Thanksgiving Day

★October 10 *(Taiiku-no-Hi)*
Health-Sports Day

Summer vacation

New Year vacation

	Second term		Third term

Autumn athletic meetings   School cultural festivals

cucumbers, egg plants ──

matsutake (a type of mushroom)

── sweet potatoes ──

pumpkins ──

── chestnuts ──

cabbages ──

── peaches ──

── apples ──

tangerines *(mikan)* ──

── grapes ──

── persimmons ──

tuna *(kuromaguro)*

── mackerel pike *(sanma)* ──

Pictorial Encyclopedia of JAPANESE CULTURE

The Soul and Heritage of Japan

国際交流基金 寄贈

With the Compliments

of

The Japan Foundation

WITHDRAWN
PROPERTY OF
CLACKAMAS COMMUNITY COLLEGE
LIBRARY

Gakken

STAFF

Editorial Consultant
Nakayama Kaneyoshi (Professor of English, Tokoha Gakuen University)
Translator
Richard De Lapp
English Language Advisors
Anne Cortese
Sekimori Gaynor (LOGOSTIKS)
Planning Advisor
Koyama Yoshihisa
Book Design
Shimada Takushi
Editorial Staff
Anzai Tatsuo
Tachibana Yukio
Kisu Production
Publishing Manager
Tachibana Yukio

Jacket photo:Woodblock print *Ichikawa Danjuro I*
as Sogano Goro uprooting a bamboo
(Tokyo National Museum Collection)

Pictorial Encyclopedia of JAPANESE CULTURE

Copyright © 1987 by GAKKEN CO., LTD.

All rights reserved, including the right to reproduce this book or portions
thereof in any form without the written permission of the publisher.

Published by GAKKEN CO., LTD.
4-40-5, Kami-ikedai, Ohta-ku, Tokyo 145, Japan

Overseas Distributor : Japan Publications Trading Co., Ltd.
P.O.Box 5030 Tokyo International, Tokyo, Japan.

Distributors:
United States : Kodansha America Inc., through Farrar, Straus & Giroux,
19 Union Square West, New York, NY 10003
Canada : Fitzhenry & Whiteside Ltd.,
195 Allstate Parkway, Markham, Ontario L3R 4T8
British Isles and the European Continent : Premier Book Marketing Ltd.,
1 Gower Street, London WC1E 6HA
Australia and New Zealand : Bookwise International, 54 Crittenden Road,
Findon 5023, South Australia
The Far East and Japan : Japan Publications Trading Co., Ltd., 1-2-1,
Sarugaku-cho, Chiyoda-ku, Tokyo 101

First edition 1987
Twenty-first printing 1994
ISBN : 0-87040-752-X
ISBN : 4-05-151315-7(in Japan)
Printed in Japan

PREFACE

Worldwide interest in Japan has mounted steadily over the past two decades in proportion to the nation's economic advancement abroad. Inevitably, the primary focus of that interest centers merely on cars, cameras, consumer electronics and other "things". There is, however, an increasing desire among people abroad to get beyond the economic realities of today's Japan and discover more about the soul that underlies the society, culture, customs and history.

Books on these aspects of Japan abound. Regrettably, their tendency to generalization does little to demystify the aura of "inscrutibility" that surrounds the Japanese image, and leaves the reader with the understandable but sadly mistaken impression that the Japanese are, after all, unique, that they do indeed form one large corporate entity, that they are, in truth, economic animals.

Japan is of course unique—just as America, Italy, and South Africa are unique. A strong characteristic of Japan's particular uniqueness is that the nation has held on to its Japaneseness despite a long history of voracious cultural borrowings. Westernized or Americanized though it may appear at first glance, Japan is, at its core, Japan, with deeply entrenched traditions and customs that underlie the surface veneer.

Being a human society, Japan is also quite capable of being understood by non-Japanese. In fact, it is on that very premise that this book was conceived and brought into its present form. In an easy-to-follow format it presents Japan's traditional culture, observances, behavioral patterns and customs, delving into their historical development to provide the reader with a fuller understanding of what constitutes the soul of this nation. To further facilitate meaningful communication with the Japanese, the book offers helpful, practical and necessary information, augmented with illustrations and pictures to enhance understanding.

This book is for all people who have an interest in Japan or who visit Japan on business, for study or for pleasure. It is also ideally suited for Japanese going abroad for similar purposes or on home-stay programs who would like their associates, friends and acquaintances to have a deeper knowledge of Japan.

CONTENTS

CREDITS

We are grateful to the following for cooperation and permission
to reproduce the photographs:

Akama Shrine, Asukamura Board of Education, Bank of Japan, Byodoin, Chishakuin,
Chokoji, Chuguji, Communications Museum, Daisenin, Enkakuji, Enryakuji, Fukuoka
Board of Education, Gakushuin University, Haga Library, Hakozakigu, Heian Shrine,
Horyuji, Idemitsu Art Gallery, Imperial Household Agency, Ise Shrine, Ishiyamadera,
Izumo Grand Shrine, Jingoji, Jishoji, Kamakura National Treasure House, Kanagawa
Prefectural Museum, Kankikoji, Kasori Shellmound Museum, Katsura Detached Palace,
Kenninji, Kishimoto Photo, Kobe City Museum, Kodaiji, Kofukuin, Kofukuji,
Koseiji, Kyodo News Service, Kyoto National Museum, Kyoto University, Nagasaki
Municipal Museum, Nara National Cultural Properties Research Institute,
National Diet Library, National Noh Theater, National Theater, Nezu Art Museum,
Meiji Village Museum, Mitoshooku, Miyagi Prefectural Library, Myokian, Omote
Senke, Osaka Castle, Oura-tenshudo, Oyamazumi Shrine, Paper Museum, Rokuonji,
Ryoanji, Sankeien, Seikado, Shibayama Haniwa Museum, Shinjuan, Shizuoka
Municipal Toro Museum, Shofukuji, Shosoin, Shugakuin Detached Palace, Suntory
Museum of Art, Takayama Museum of Local History, Taharacho Board of Education,
The Fuji Bank Ltd, The Hatakeyama Collection, The Sanwa Bank Ltd, The Tokai Bank
Ltd, The Tokugawa Reimeikai Foundation, The Yasukuni Shrine, Todaiji, Tohoku
University, Tokeiji, Tokyo National Museum, Tokyo University, Tokyo University
of Art, Toshodaiji, Toshogu Shrine, Tsunanmachi Board of Education, Tsurugaoka
Hachiman Shrine, Yakushiji, Yamatobunkakan, Zuisenji, others.

THE LAND OF THE RISING SUN

Japanese mythology declares that the deities were born amidst the chaotic time when heaven and earth had just separated. Izanagi and Izanami were respectively the seventh male and female gods. Both of them thrust a halberd from the Bridge of Heaven into the sea. As they withdrew it, droplets trickling off the halberd formed an island. Izanagi and Izanami descended to it and brought forth island after island: Japan was created.

Izanami gives birth to various gods, but is burned to death while delivering the god of fire. After seeing her dead body, Izanagi proceeds to a river to purify himself, whereupon three more deities are born. One is Amaterasu-o-mikami, the sun goddess and queen of the divine country Takamagahara. Another is Tsukuyomi-no-mikoto, the moon god and the ruler of the kingdom of darkness. The third is the rogue Susanoo-no-mikoto, the tyrant of the seas.

Amaterasu-o-mikami sends her grandson Ninigi-no-mikoto down from heaven to the mountain pass called Takachiho to rule over the islands of Japan. His progeny beget the first Japanese Emperor.

Japanese myths are recorded in two historic works of the 8th century: *Kojiki* (Record of Ancient Matters), and *Nihon Shoki* (Chronicles of Japan). Though written with the intent of furthering the cause of the Imperial House, the myths also afford a good understanding of how the people of the time saw the world and nature.

▶ **Susanoo-no-mikoto Slaying the Serpent** Japanese mythology relates the following story about Susanoo-no-mikoto. He was such a wild fellow that he was driven out of the divine land of Takamagahara by his sister Amaterasu-o-mikami. He descended to the land of Izumo (present-day Shimane prefecture). Walking along the upper reaches of a river he came upon a young girl crying. When asked why, she explained that the great serpent, Yamata-no-orochi came each year to devour a maiden and that her turn was now at hand. Susanoo-no-mikoto thereupon tricked the serpent into getting drunk, slew him, and married the maiden.

Each autumn in the Izumo area a dance based on this story is performed, one segment of which is shown in the photo.

SHRINES

Shinto—the way of the gods—is the name given to the simple faith possessed by the ancient Japanese. Whether it can also be termed a religion is a matter of debate, for Shinto has no particular teachings or dogmas. It is just a belief in the power of spirits thought to be in man and in elements of nature. This spritual power is what the Japanese call *kami*.

Kami could be all of one's deceased relatives or all of the dead. The sun, mountains, wind, rain, rocks, trees and other natural phenomena were also believed to be indwelt by *kami*. If worshipped, *kami* would be benevolent towards people, but provoked to wrath and possible calamity when neglected. People therefore chose to worship *kami*. That, in brief, is the basis of the faith referred to as Shinto.

Because the ancient Japanese deified and directly worshipped mountains, trees, even the sun as they were found in nature, religious edifices were unnecessary. Eventually, however, structures were built in places where *kami* could be worshipped. Each structure was given a specific name to show its purpose, such as *haiden* for the building where worshippers offer prayers, or *honden* for the building that contains the symbol (often a mirror) of the enshrined deity. Collectively, these structures are called *jinja* (shrines).

▲*Torii* *Torii* mark the entrance to a shrine, indicating that what lies ahead is ground sacred to the gods.

◀**Kasuga Grand Shrine** The family shrine of the politically powerful Fujiwara clan that held power at court from the 7th to the 12th centuries. The shrine was begun around the 8th century, but the present *honden* (main building) dates back about 200 years.

▲ *Goshinboku* (**god-tree**)   A rice-straw rope (*shimenawa*) tied around the trunk of a tree indicates the spot where the divinities descend to earth.

◄ **Aerial View of Izumo Grand Shrine** This shrine is credited to Okuninushi-no-mikoto, the fabulous ruler of the Izumo region in the mythological age. Along with the Ise Grand Shrine on the next page, it is one of the oldest shrines in Japan.

◄ (above) **Shinto Priest at Prayer** The priest offers prayers of celebration (*norito*) to the gods.

◄ (below)   **Priest Making Fire** Fire to be used at shrines is created the natural way through friction.

▲ *Miko* (**shrine maidens**) **at a Wedding**   *Miko* originally played an intercessionary role between man and the deities, relaying the divine will.

9

▲**Approach to Ise Shrine** Across the bridge is the *torii* that signals the shrine entrance. In former times, worshippers first purified themselves in the river.

▶**Main Hall of Ise Shrine** Ise Shrine is divided into "inner" and "outer" shrines. The inner shrine is sacred to Amaterasu-o-mikami, the deity of the Imperial House. Like Izumo Grand Shrine, Ise is one of the oldest shrines in Japan. It is rebuilt every 20 years, but always retaining the same design and form. The most recent rebuilding was in 1973. Despite its dedication to the legendary deity of the Imperial House, the building is a plain structure of Japanese cypress. It is precisely this simplicity, however, that so stirs the faith among the Japanese.

▼**Imperial Messenger to Ise Shrine** At the forefront is a female member of the Imperial House. The robes of the entourage are fashioned according to those worn at court until 120 years ago.

HARMONIZING WITH NATURE

Earthenware, called Jomon ("rope print") after its decorative patterns, began to be used in Japan some 10,000 years ago. What appear to be the prototypes of the Japanese and their language also fall within the Jomon period: 10,000 B. C.~300 B. C.

Some of the pottery of mid-Jomon times has decorative flame-like shapes that seem to leap as if in praise of the might of heaven and earth, suggesting that for the people of the period, pottery-making was also a way to express a heightened artistic awareness.

A temperate climate has long made the Japanese view nature as a giver of blessings. Harmonizing with nature and becoming one with it is a feeling that lies at the root of Japanese spiritual life.

▲**Earthen Mask** It was probably used at rites invoking the earth's bounty.

▼**Restored Pit Dwellings** They were dug to a depth of about 50cm.

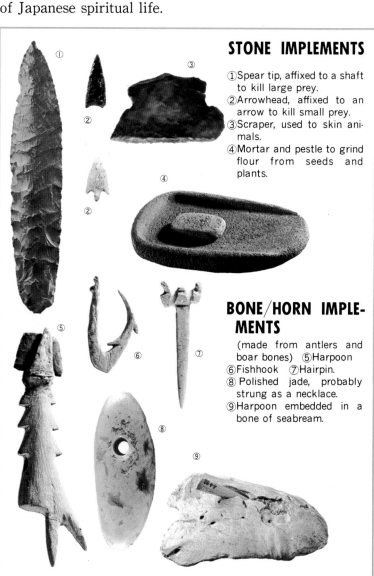

STONE IMPLEMENTS

①Spear tip, affixed to a shaft to kill large prey.
②Arrowhead, affixed to an arrow to kill small prey.
③Scraper, used to skin animals.
④Mortar and pestle to grind flour from seeds and plants.

BONE/HORN IMPLEMENTS

(made from antlers and boar bones) ⑤Harpoon ⑥Fishhook ⑦Hairpin.
⑧ Polished jade, probably strung as a necklace.
⑨Harpoon embedded in a bone of seabream.

▲One of the oldest pieces of Jomon earthenware.

▲Sculpture-like pottery from around 5000 B. C. with elaborate ornamentation suggestive of flames. It may have been used as a storage container for precious grains.

*In an age when life was always exposed to nature's dangers, a simple faith in magic was practiced for self-protection and good harvests.

▶A clay figure in a human-like form was probably thought capable of warding off evil spirits. Tablets and stone idols were used for similar purposes.

▼**Skeleton** The classic posture for burial in the Jomon period, with arms and legs folded. Theories abound as to why.

13

FARMING-BASED GROUPISM

The technique of wet-rice cultivation came from China and Korea around 300 B. C. Although hunting continued, the onset of farming made life more settled and regular crop production changed Japanese life. Because rice cultivation required more of a group effort than hunting, a more closely-knit social order was necessary. Consequently, the farming culture was the basis for the Japanese tendency to collective action.

Concurrently from China and Korea came metalware of bronze and iron. Bronzeware was mainly used for religious rites, whereas iron was used for making tools.

Earthenware went from the rough vigor of the Jomon epoch to a simpler design. These two tendencies later formed the Japanese aesthetic sense.

The Yayoi period (300 B. C.~300 A. D.) is named for the Tokyo site of the discovery of its pottery. The intrinsic character of Japanese culture flourished as the beliefs, customs and folkways of this period's predominantly agricultural society spread.

▲**Yayoi Earthenware**   First unearthed in Yayoi, Tokyo.

▲**Aqueduct Remains**   A waterway that ran between two rows of wooden supports. (Toro, Shizuoka prefecture)
◀**Pit Dwelling Remains**   Built atop mounded earth. Small center holes were for posts. (Toro)

▼**Reconstructed Pit Dwelling**

◀**Bronze Sword**
A widebladed sword made in Japan for ceremonial use.

▶**Bell-shaped Bronze**
Many were buried in small groups in mountains and elsewhere away from settlements, perhaps as treasures to be hidden and saved from marauding groups.

Stone and Bronze Tools

①Stone knife ②Stone ax
③-⑤Bronze spade. Unearthed at sites in Fukuoka prefecture.

Wood Tools

Farm and everyday tools from a site in Toro.
①Rake
②Ladle
③Fire drill (base)
④Fire drill (bow)
⑤Footwear
⑥One-legged folding table

▲(above) **Cutting Stone** Fingers hook under cord run through holes. Thumb presses one rice ear at a time against the cutting edge.

▲(below) **Fire Drill** Vertical motion of the bar rotates the stick in the hollow of the wood base to create friction and flame.

▼Threshing scene depicted on bell-shaped bronze.

▼**Bronze Mirror** A symbol of the sun, not an object for viewing one's face. A prized treasure held by a chief. Lettering is visible on the back.

▲Haniwa These figures of clay were placed around and atop the burial mound, probably as tableaus in clay of the life of the deceased.

BURIAL MOUND CULTURE

High-mounded graves that first developed in western Japan around 400 A.D. to serve as burial places for political administrators are called *kofun*.

The largest is the mound in Osaka for Emperor Nintoku. Its 486-meter length exceeds even the largest of the pyramids. It would have taken 1,000 workers a day four years to complete it. Only personages of powerful clans had the wherewithal to build such colossal tombs.

The mounds were surrounded by moats and topped with *haniwa* (clay figures of people, houses and animals).

In addition to the body, mirrors and ornaments were buried in the *kofun*. Equestrian paraphernalia increased as the eras evolved. *Kofun* interiors were likely regarded as belonging to the afterlife.

Around the 5th century, characters for writing, called *kan* (China) *ji* (letter) were introduced from China. Many express meaning through form, such as "川" for river or "木" for tree.

▶**Restored Goshikizuka Tomb**   Many of the old tombs extant today are covered with trees. Those in ancient times were entirely covered with stones.

▲ **Miko** Interceded between man and heaven to convey divine will.

◄ **Tomb of Emperor Nintoku** The largest tomb in Japan. It is square at the front and round at the rear. Other tombs come in cubes and domes.

▶ **Ear Pendants** Metal with complex design.

◄ **Magatama** "Curved jewels" sometimes worn as necklaces.

▼ **Horse Fittings** Bridle bit (left & right) and ornaments for rear flanks (center).

▼ **Armor of the Period** The burial of military and equestrian paraphernalia suggests an age in which much fighting occured over unification attempts.

◄ **Decorated Tomb** Letters and figures in geometric patterns decorate the stone chamber walls. Many such tombs are found in Kyushu, southernmost major island of Japan.

BUDDHISM'S PROFOUND IMPACT

After its arrival in Japan from Korea in 538 A. D., Buddhism ignited a struggle among powerful clans. Victory by its supporters led to its rapid spread and the building of temples; Horyuji (temple) in Nara is a classic example.

Because Buddhism was the first systematic thought carried to Japan, it influenced all subsequent art, architecture, literature, technology and thought. Temples became centers of higher learning from the continent, and their architecture and statuary captured the hearts and minds of the Japanese.

▲ **Prince Shotoku** The age's foremost Buddhist thinker to whom the erection of the Horyuji is attributed. A political reformer and regent to the first Empress, Suiko.

◀ **Aerial View of the Horyuji** the world's oldest wooden structure. A number of national treasures of Buddhist statuary and traditional crafts are housed here.

▲ **Miroku (a future Buddha)** Seemingly lost in contemplation, its facial expression imparts a captivating sense of delicate gentleness. (Chuguji)

◀ **Buddhist Trinity of The Horyuji's Golden Hall** The faint smile is referred to as "the archaic smile."

Decapitated Buddha
Though only the head remains, the robust but gentle-looking features exhibit great charm. (Kofukuji)

▲**Wall Painting at the Horyuji (Copy)** Clearly shows artistic influences from Ghandara, Pakistan.

▲**Yakushiji Pagoda** What appear to be six roofs are actually three due to an architectural technique called *mokoshi*. Pagodas were originally built to house relics of Shaka, the founder of Buddhism. Visible from afar, they now symbolize temples.

●Takamatsu Burial Mound

While ancient tombs in Japan show influences from China and Korea, differences among them also exist. Distinctive only to Chinese and Korean tombs is the presence of wall paintings depicting the lives of their rulers.

Decorated tombs do exist (see p. 17), but the decorations are extreme abstractions void of human representation. In 1972, however, a tomb was discovered in Asuka, Nara that has realistic wall paintings. The tomb is called the Takamatsu Burial Mound.

The paintings (see photo, right), show groups of men and women, plus animals that symbolize the deities of the four directions. The tomb also contains human remains, wooden coffins of lacquer overlaid with goldleaf, bronze mirrors and other items.

Direct influences from China and Korea are revealed by the artifacts and painting techniques. The tomb itself is thought to date from the mid-7th to 8th century.

THE NARA CAPITAL AND THE GREAT BUDDHA

In 710 A.D. Japan's capital was moved to Nara. Nara was modeled after an early Chinese capital; it extended 4.2 km east to west and 4.7 km north and south. Previous capitals were smaller. Nara was the first full-scale capital. The 70 or so years following its construction are called the Nara period.

Because the emperors of this period were devout Buddhists, Buddhistic culture flourished. The statue in the Todaiji is a classic example. Emperor Shomu built it in the hope of propagating Buddhism as a means in stabilizing the country. It is the world's largest statue of cast metal. Yet the Buddhism of this age stayed within the nobility and did not spread to the masses.

▲**The Todaiji Buddha**   Wars and earthquakes damaged the original. Today's statue dates to the late 1600s and stands 14.9m (originally 16m).

▲**Lecture Hall of Toshodaiji**   Once a part of government offices within the palace grounds. Despite considerable repairs, it is a good model of the original.

◀**Site of Former Palace**   Excavated in the north-central part of the old capital. Yields include items of daily use. The site is now a public park.

▲**Todaiji**   The Hall of the Great Buddha is visible above the treetops.

▶ **Emperor Shomu**   He used the power of Buddhism to reign, built temples throughout the country and had the Todaiji and Buddha constructed.
◀**Zochoten**   One of the four protective deities of Buddhism.

▼**Unglazed Tableware**   Simple and unadorned.

THE SHOSOIN

A treasure house located near the Todaiji in Nara. Its three repositories (north, central, south), were built around 752 A.D. and house some 10,000 items. Many were the personal possessions of Emperor Shomu, while others belonged to the nobility of the Nara period. Still others came from abroad and attest to Japan's cultural contact with the countries such as China, India, Persia some 1200 years ago.

▶ **Temple/shrine register:** Lists descriptions, purposes and givers of gifts.

Treasures of the Shosoin

① Incense burner. Used to transfer scents to clothing.
② Pedestal for incense burner.
③ Inkstone.
④ Vessel for medicine.
⑤ Wooden *go* board with Persian pattern evident on sides.
⑥ Writing brushes, with tips intact.
⑦ Penknives.
⑧ Court lady in Chinese-style dress. Face, robes, background done in feathers.
⑨ Long-handled censer for carrying incense to Buddhist images.
⑩ Lion head used in court music.
⑪ Mask used in court music.
⑫ Belt inlaid with lapis lazuli from Afghanistan.
⑬ Tableware of flint glass.
⑭ Five-stringed *biwa* with Persian motif.

BEAUTIFUL OLD KYOTO

Though Buddhism in the Nara period was state-supported and Buddhistic culture flourished, serious abuses occurred when the religion grew so strong that it could exert influence on politics.

Emperor Kanmu therefore founded a new capital in Kyoto in 794 A.D. He named the capital Heian-kyo; he wanted peace (hei) and stability (an) permanently secured. Larger than Nara, it stretched 4.5 km east to west and 5.3 km north and south.

His dreams were not realized, however, as the political war between the nobility raged. Nevertheless, Kyoto continued to develop, and for some 1000 years held supreme authority as capital and cultural center of the nation. Today it is renown as a city of historic traditions, beautiful temples and as a mecca for tourists.

◀**Heian Shrine** Built in 1895 to commemorate the moving of the capital by Emperor Kanmu to Kyoto 1000 years earlier. Its architecture is adapted from a building that was once the capital's political hub.

▶**Marketplace in the Old Capital** There were two: one in the east sector, the other in the west.

▲**Government vs. Northeast Troops** Evidence that the Kyoto government had yet to control the entire nation.

▲**Security Forces in Kyoto** Units patrolled the streets to maintain law and order.

▲**Aoi Festival**　Held every May 15th, this famous Kyoto festival vividly recalls the splendor of the city's past.

●ESOTERIC BUDDHISM AND SECRET RITES

The excesses of the established Buddhist sects were curbed with the arrival on the religious scene of the two priests, Saicho and Kukai. Each had gone to China at the turn of the 9th century to study Buddhism, and upon returning had founded a new sect. Together the two sects, Saicho's Tendai and Kukai's Shingon, became the mainstream of esoteric Buddhism in Japan.

This type of Buddhism had had its start in 7th-8th century India and held that the most profound teachings of Buddha were to be found in secret rites. Through intense prayer, priests were to strive to establish a connection with the spirits present in the universe. To gain this ability to become one with creation required secluding oneself in serene surroundings in the mountains and practicing rigorous self-denial and austerities. Hence the epithet "Mountain Buddhism" was applied to this new school as opposed to the "urban Buddhism" of the older Nara sects.

Such acts of prayer designed to grasp the secrets of the universe contain simultaneously a very primitive aspect and a highly spiritual aspect, a dichotomy that is one of the characteristics making up the culture of Japan.

▶(above) **Mt. Koya**　Here Kukai built the Kongobuji as the headquarters of his sect. There are many esoteric temples deep in the mountains.

▶(below) **Enryakuji**　Saicho built this temple on Mt. Hiei as the head temple of the Tendai Sect.

THE LIFE-STYLE OF THE NOBILITY

The Fujiwara clan was of the nobility and had secured political power in Kyoto by intrigue, taking possession of major offices.

Accompanying their autonomy was the practice of giving their daughters in marriage to emperors as a means of appointing themselves to high positions.

In their disdain for war, nobles immersed themselves in formalities and rituals that required ornate attire. The nobility lived lavishly in this manner on huge incomes from their country estates. Its life-styles created the standard for elegance and culture.

The strong influence Tang China had once exerted during the Nara period was digested and Japanized into truly Japanese models as Japanese aestheticism and culture were fostered.

▲(above) **Temple Visits** More was involved than religious piety, as such visits constituted the greatest recreation enjoyed by the nobility.

▲(below) **Playing *Go*** Court ladies compete to see who can cover more of the 361 places on the board with stones of their color, either black or white.

◄**Nobleman's Estate** The manor (*shinden*) is connected by corridor to the family quarters and to those for retainers. A pond big enough for pleasure-boating is in the garden.

▲**Football** A leather ball is kept in the air by kicking.

▲**Cock-fighting** A spring ritual in which cocks are goaded into fighting.

Musical Diversion Nobles engage in pleasant conversation (above), while on the pond a boat carrying musicians glides by.

Noblewoman in Full Dress The wearer's taste was judged by the colors and hues of the layered clothing visible at the sleeve tips.

Phoenix Hall of the Byodoin This beautiful structure was built in Uji, Kyoto, by the Fujiwaras as a representation of what they hoped to find in the hereafter.

Nobleman in Full Dress A peaked hat, and a wood scepter to maintain dignity.

Nobleman's Carriage Shown here is one for the sole use of the Emperor, Empress or others of the highest rank.

THE WORLD OF *GENJI MONOGATARI*

Genji Monogatari (The Tale of Genji) is the most famous work of Japanese literature known abroad thanks in great measure to the English translation of Arthur Waley and, more recently, that of Edward Seidensticker. The original book was written in the early 11th century and contained 54 chapters. Its author was Murasaki Shikibu, a lady-in-waiting to the daughter of Fujiwara Michinaga, who was a high-ranking and powerful figure at court.

The story concerns the amorous adventures of Hikaru Genji, a handsome young noble of imperial descent. In the age in which the story takes place it was not the custom among the upper strata of the nobility to practice monogamy. Instead, a gentleman would visit his lover's house, or simply set up quarters for a lady who had taken his fancy and given her consent, and then call on her at nightfall. The life of Hikaru Genji follows the same pattern, but despite his romantic involvement with various ladies, he is unable to forsake past loves.

Monono aware, the dominant aesthetic that runs through the story, is what the Japanese identify as one of pathos, which expresses the feelings that arise from deep stirrings within the heart as we sense the transience of every event.

The original book was written in a Japanese script called *kana*—phonetic symbols developed by the Japanese based on Chinese characters. This is yet another reason for the important position the book occupies in the cultural history of Japan.

Inspired by the beautiful love story, many an artist has put brush to canvas so that there exists a whole genre of pictures based on the story, the so-called "Genji pictures."

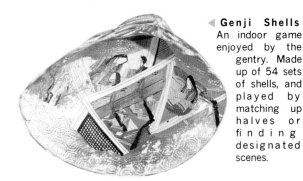

◀ **Genji Shells** An indoor game enjoyed by the gentry. Made up of 54 sets of shells, and played by matching up halves or finding designated scenes.

▶ **Genji and Child** The child was born to Genji's wife but not sired by Genji. Though painfully aware of the situation, Genji determined to raise him as his own. The picture is from the *Genji Scroll*, painted in the early 12th century.

▲ **Murasaki Shikibu** The daughter of a provincial governor. She later became a lady-in-waiting at court, where her book *Genji Monogatari* proved popular. Fujiwara Michinaga, the most powerful man then at court, had Murasaki become tutor to his daughter, the Empress Shoshi.

▲ **The Aristocracy Amusing Themselves** A scene of members of the nobility enjoying the hospitality of the Emperor. Boats sail about the pond (above and below). At center left are two dancing figures. Painted between the end of the 16th century and the beginning of the 17th.

BUDDHIST STATUES

Buddhism is more of a philosophical system of thought centering on the principle of mercy than it is a religion. Its teachings center on how to solve or overcome the problems of life and death, and hold that all things change.

Statues of Shaka, the founder of Buddhism, are objects of worship, as are various other deities sacred to Buddhism. Over the centuries they have come to be stylized into various forms, as shown here:

① Nyorai——A manifestation of the enlightened Buddha.

② Bosatsu (Bodhisattva)——A deity in the process of becoming a Buddha (Nyorai). The highest of Shaka's disciples.

③ Tenbu——Deities in India prior to the advent of Buddhism. They subsequently became believers in and protectors of Buddhism.

④ Myoo——A deity empowered by Nyorai to overcome evil.

⑤ Rakan——Buddha's disciples and high priests.

Distinguishing which deity is which is no easy task. Even the positions and shapes of the arms, hands and fingers have individual significance. The only ones easy to identify are the Nyorai, for they are simply clad in one-layered garments and are unadorned with personal ornamentation such as crowns or necklaces. Having cast off all worldly possessions, they devote themselves wholeheartedly to ascetic practices, a sight that draws the sympathy and admiration of suffering humanity.

▶**Yakushi Triad** This trio of Buddhist statues at the Yakushiji in Nara dates back to the 7th century. In the center in a sitting position is a Nyorai-type statue called Yakushi Nyorai, the healing Buddha. To its left and right are Nikko Bosatsu and Gakko Bosatsu, two typical bosatsu-style attendants. Often there are statues of Kannon (Goddess of Mercy) on both sides of a Nyorai statue, and the arrangement is called a triad. In the case of Yakushi Nyorai, however, Nikko and Gakko bosatsu always appear. Since Nyorai statues represent the enlightened Buddha they are unadorned and in simple dress. Kannon, representing Shaka (Buddha) in youth before enlightenment, has a crown and ornamentation.

THE RISE OF THE SAMURAI

The word *samurai* comes from a verb meaning "attend upon a noble." This the samurai did, serving and guarding them and fighting in their stead in wartime.

The provinces politically decayed while the nobles luxuriated in Kyoto. Leading families encroached upon neighboring lands and in some cases attacked government offices. As always, samurai were sent to restore order. Their power accordingly increased and they began to make their voices heard. Two particularly strong clans were the Genji and the Heike.

The two clans were rivals, and at one time the Heike actually curbed the power of the Fujiwara and seized control. However, because the Heike had made their headquarters in Kyoto, they themselves became effete and in turn were defeated by the Genji clan under Minamoto Yoritomo. Later, in 1192, Yoritomo established a military government in Kamakura which eventually ushered in an era centered on the warrior class rather than on the nobility.

▲**Early Warrior and Attendants** The image of the fighting samurai is not yet evident.

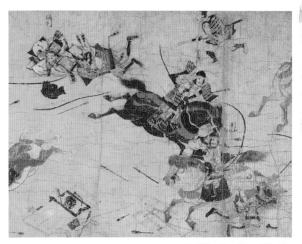

▲**Battle in the Northeast** This portion of the country was particularly powerful and unheedful of the central government. The Genji were sent to rectify that.

◄**Torching a Manor** A power-struggle between the nobility and the samurai arose in the latter half of the 12th century. The Heike, led by Taira Kiyomori, were victorious and held control for 25 years thereafter.

Itsukushima Refurbished and enlarged by Kiyomori to make it the patron shrine of the Heike clan. (Hiroshima prefecture)

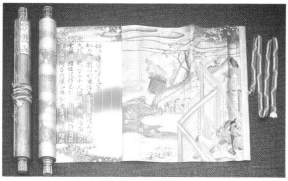

Sutra Presented to Itsukushima shrine by the Heike in hopes of gaining glory for their clan. Though descended from samurai they followed aristocratic customs.

The Fall of the Heike The clan was overthrown by the Genji. Antoku, the 8-year-old Emperor of Heike descent, goes to his death in his grandmother's arms.

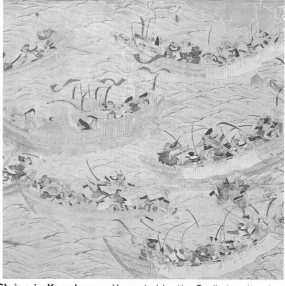

Hachiman Shrine in Kamakura Venerated by the Genji clan. Its simplicity contrasts sharply with the patron shrine of the Heike at Itsukushima.

Minamoto Yoritomo Became Shogun after defeating the Heike and set up a government in Kamakura, far from the Kyoto nobility.

ARMS AND ARMOR

Japanese arms and armor gradually developed in accordance with times and necessities.

For example, early Japanese swords were straight and only used for thrusting until they became curved in the 9th century in order to be used for slashing.

Full armors were perfected in the 10th century for protection of mounted commanders. Commanders also needed doublets and protectors previously used only by foot-soldiers, because in the 13th-14th centuries tactics of warfare intensified to group onslaughts by sword. European influences followed the introduction of firearms in the mid-1500s.

The Tokugawa reign was a 200-year war-free era that permitted extravagance to flourish; instruments of war were embellished in color, craftsmanship and fine design and became appreciated as works of art.

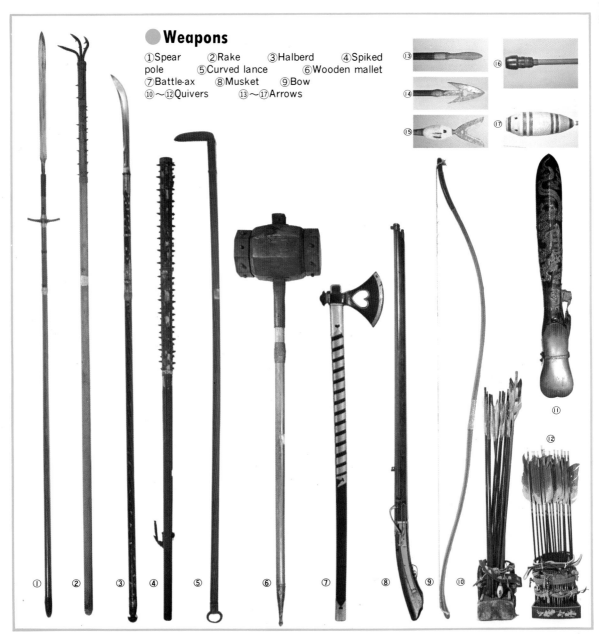

● **Weapons**
①Spear ②Rake ③Halberd ④Spiked pole ⑤Curved lance ⑥Wooden mallet ⑦Battle-ax ⑧Musket ⑨Bow ⑩～⑫Quivers ⑬～⑰Arrows

▲ **Todaiji South Gate**   Done in Chinese style. The temple was destroyed by fire in fighting between the Genji and Heike clans, but was rebuilt in 1195.

▶ **Laboring to Build a Temple**

◀ **Shariden of the Enkakuji** Done in the Chinese *So* style with sharply curved roof edges.

Mongol Invasion and the Kamikaze   Mongol forces attacked Japan in 1274 and 1281. In the midst of each of the two battles a typhoon struck and delivered fatal blows to the Mongols. This *kami* (god) *kaze* (wind) convinced many that Japan was under divine protection.

Types of Swords

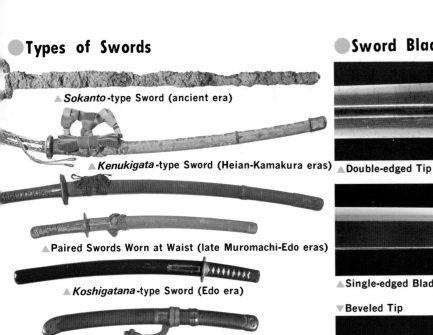

▲ *Sokanto*-type Sword (ancient era)

▲ *Kenukigata*-type Sword (Heian-Kamakura eras)

▲ Paired Swords Worn at Waist (late Muromachi-Edo eras)

▲ *Koshigatana*-type Sword (Edo era)

▲ *Wakizashi*-type Sword (Edo era)

◀ *Aikuchi*-style Dagger (Edo era)

Sword Blades

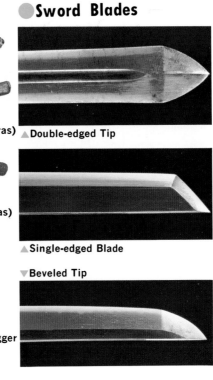

▲ Double-edged Tip

▲ Single-edged Blade

▼ Beveled Tip

Sword G[uards]

Originally made [to pro-]
tect the hand[...]
eventually for[...]
decorative beau[ty...]

Types of Armor

▲ Clay Figure In Doublet

STEPS IN PUTTING ON ARMOR

cap (eboshi)

hitatare

shin guards

loincloth and silk garment

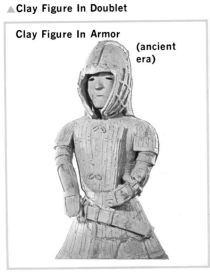

▲ Clay Figure In Armor (ancient era)

Full Armor (8th~19th centuries)

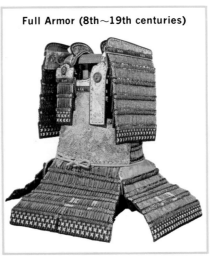

Torso Wrap-around (8th-19th cent[uries)]

● Unusual Helmets

to pro-
s but
their
y.

Manufacture advanced in the 1600s, helmets becoming ornamental as well as protective.

▲Armorer's Shop (around the middle of the 16th century)

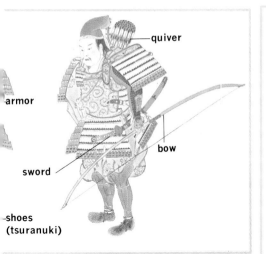

quiver

armor

sword

bow

—shoes
(tsuranuki)

Armor of the 16th to 19th centuries

uries)

Abdominal Protector (14th-19th centuries)

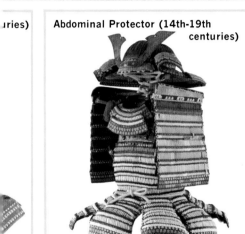

THE CULTURE OF THE WARRIOR CLASS

Preaching A priest delivers a sermon to those in search of salvation.

The Kamakura military established a government of acknowledged power, but culturally lacking the finesse of Kyoto.

Kamakura's culture evolved from its military's constant readiness, its pride, and its awareness that true power lay with them. The soldiers were virile and valorous; the city was teeming with activity and force which sharply contrasted with the grace and elegance that epitomized the Kyoto nobility.

The atmospheres of Kyoto and Kamakura respectively created the two currents that comprise the stream of Japanese aesthetics —the elegant, the quiet, the refined, versus the rugged and the vigorous.

Buddhism, too, went from complex dogma to teachings understandable to all, and in doing so became internalized and Japanized.

Yabusame Shooting at a target from horseback. Such competitions honed military skills. The contest can still be seen in Kamakura today.

Warrior's Home Plain in comparison with a nobleman's manor. Above the gate is a defensive fortification.

▲ ***Ryutoki*** A sculpture alive with the earthy humor of the commoners.
▶ ***Kongorikishi*** In its powerful sturdiness this sculpture well symbolizes the vigor inherent in the culture of the warrior class.

▼ ***Suigetsu* Goddess of Mercy** Buddhist statues invited intense prayer and faith, but until this one atop a dais of rocks appeared it was rare for one to project a sense of being at ease.

WABI-AESTHETIC IDEAL

Two cultures of Muromachi period: the sumptuous one exemplified by the Golden Pavilion (Kinkakuji) and the elegantly refined one exemplified by the Silver Pavilion (Ginkakuji). China and Zen Buddhism exerted a profound influence, the arts flourished and, along with industry and education, spread to the clergy and military under the autonomous rule of the warring *Daimyo*.

▲**Mask for Kyogen** A comic interlude between *Noh* plays.
▼**Noh Theater** Early *Noh* Audience. With the patronage of the Shoguns, playwrights raised Noh to a peak of refinement.

◀**China-mania** Imports like this lacquered tray were highly prized.

▲**Noh Mask** Noh is a type of mask theater. The masks are designed to express both joy and sadness, depending on the requirements of the scene.

▲**Kinkakuji** Destroyed by fire in 1950: rebuilt in 1955.
▼The Ryoanji's roofed wall is made of oil-impregnated soil; thatched shingles of the overhang have been restored.

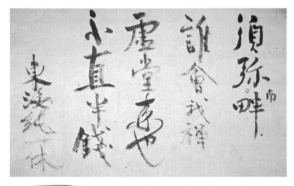

▲**Five-Temple Literature** refers collectively to the copious output of writings by Zen priests (mainly of the Rinzai Sect) which, during the Muromachi period, contributed much to the literary arts and learning. (writing of Priest Ikkyu.)
◀**Celadon Porcelain from China.**

▲Room used by Shogun Yo-shimasa as a study.
▶Ginkakuji   A chapel above, a study below. Death halted the Shogun's plans to gild it with silver.

▲Flower Arrangement Forms were laid down in this period and in vogue among all classes. (page in 1529 manual.)

▼Eating habits and diet improved in this period. Daily meals rose to three; foodstuffs increased; culinary arts advanced; Japanese cuisine became fixed.

■ Tea Ceremony   Implements range from whisks to kettles. Choice Chinese bowls were often used. The system of appreciating both the tea and the implements dates from this period.

▲Tea bowl from China
▼Ink Painting Winter scene from a scroll by Sesshu, who Japanized the original Chinese technique.

▲Maki-e a unique Japanese art also exported to China. (maki-e box favored by Shogun Yoshimasa.)

▲Chinese Kettle

THE BEAUTY OF NOH

Noh, based on an old folk art and perfected in the 14th century, is one of the oldest traditional arts in Japan. It could well be called a kind of dance-drama performed through song and dance.

The Noh player speaks and chants his part, while scenic description is provided by a chorus of 8 or 10 persons. A story teller gives the story development, and there is musical accompaniment by one flute and two, sometimes three, drums.

Another of the singularities of Noh is its mask drama. Through the use of swift changes the performer can instantly transform from, say, a young woman to an evil spirit.

The central characters in a Noh play are not ordinary human beings. In some cases they are not human at all. Lost souls, crazed women, evil spirits, even plants and animals are some of the supernatural characters that stalk through this theater of the fantastic. Stripping away the veil of life's conventionalities, Noh reveals through dance the web of unfulfilled resentments behind the face of man, the crushing agony of the dark desires that smolder in the deep recesses of the human heart. It is, so to speak, a drama of human alienation.

Noh brims with deep insights into the human spirit. What we come to sense within its simplified expressions and symbolic movements is a highly esoteric awareness of beauty. More than just a traditional type of theater, Noh has about it much of the avant-garde.

▲▶ **The Noh Stage**   The Noh stage, unlike the standard pictureframe type in the West, allows for an audience on its left in addition to its front. Props are minimal, and scenery is a single pine painted on a backdrop. Performances take place towards the rear part of the stage to the accompaniment of a flute and various-sized drums. Story narrations are sung by chanters at stage right. Upper photo shows a scene from "Shakkyo Old Style", with two lions frolicking among the peonies. At right is a scene from "Kakitsubata", a play about a woman longing for her dead lover.

▲ **Takigi Noh**   Fire consecrated to the gods is made by burning *takigi* (firewood). *Takigi* Noh originally meant "Noh performances for the gods". Now it refers to outdoor performances by torchlight.

▷ **Noh Robes**   Elaborately designed and carefully made.

● Noh Masks

● Kyogen Masks

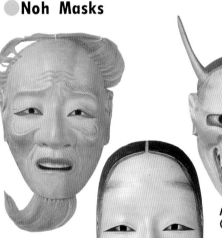

Ko-ushi
(old man)

Hannya
(devil)

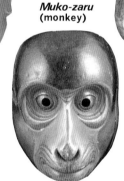

Waka-onna
(young woman)

Muko-zaru
(monkey)

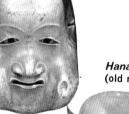

Fukure
(old woman)

Hana-hiki
(old man)

▷ **Kyogen Performance**   "Kyogen" literally means "deviant words". It is a farce-comedy performed between Noh plays. It sometimes makes use of masks. Pictured is a scene from "Hanago", in which a man boasts of having come to see his lover, not recognizing that the person in night-clothes is actually his wife.

43

ZEN AND MEDITATION

Zen, as a way for Zen Buddhists to attain spiritual enlightenment, is a practical method of soul-searching that stresses the practice of meditation. To sit in meditation, and through the stilling of the mind to try to grasp the truth of the universe (the nothingness of the absolute) is by no means restricted to Buddhists or priests. Practitioners include business people, athletes, and many people in other lands.

Zen's fundamental teaching is that in the pursuit of truth one must not rely on words. That is, truth transcends the limits set by rational thought, so one must grasp truth directly through meditation. Since man has a latent intuitive power, the object of meditation is to rouse it by turning the mind over to its unconscious, involuntary actions.

Japanese priests who studied Zen in China brought it to Japan in the 12th-13th centuries where it spread mainly among the military class. Japanese culture's strong preference for the meditative and the silent is due greatly to the influence of Zen. Stone gardens, ink paintings, the tea ceremony, and flower arrangement are all cultural heirs of the Zen spirit. Often-heard complaints that the Japanese are not logical in what they say or that it is difficult to tell what a Japanese is thinking may well be attributed to the many points on which Japanese thought harmonizes with the spirit of Zen.

▲**Dogen** Zen teachings were brought to Japan by Eisai and Dogen in the 12th and 13th centuries.

▶ (above) **Monks in Meditation** Done once in the early morning, once again in the evening. When concentration falters, a trainer (*jikido*) strikes the monk's shoulder sharply with an oakwood pole to correct him.

▶ (below) **Novitiates Clean the Temple** Cleaning and cooking are important practices in the search for enlightenment.

Ink Painting   Nature's grandeur is captured by simple ink-shadings. Ink paintings reflect the Zen spirit of quiet and meditation. (Ama-no-Hashidate by Sesshu; early 16th century.)

A Rock Garden   Gardens that liken stones to mountains and islands, sand to seas, are, like Zen, seeing the world in a grain of sand. (Daiseninshoin, Kyoto)

Zen Monks Seeking Alms   Chanting sutras while making the rounds of homes to solicit alms is an important part of training for monks.

PUBLIC ENTERTAINMENTS

Towns had mainly flourished around seats of the government. But in the 15th-16th centuries towns in their true sense formed through the commerce and industry of their inhabitants. Burghers were merchants who enjoyed self-rule in these towns. These bourgeois began or revived the Doll Festival, the Star Festival, the Gion Festival of Kyoto, and created much of the liveliness of contemporary town life.

Enjoying a puppet show

Gion Festival in Kyoto

Ritual dance with a lion's mask

Excursion to view the maple leaves
Net-fishing in a river

Lute player

●Fairy Tale Books

Easy-to-read, illustrated books for the bourgeois. Books prior to the 15th-16th centuries were only for nobles, clergymen or samurai. These delightful animal, ghost, or success stories form the basis for many of today's well-loved nursery tales.

▶ Scene from a tale about a sparrow.

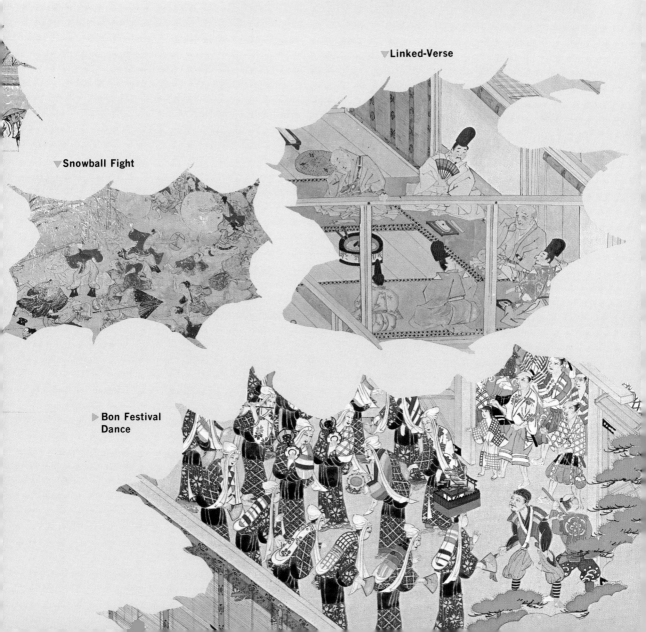

▼ Linked-Verse

▼ Snowball Fight

▶ Bon Festival Dance

CURRENCY
OLD AND NEW

⑪Keicho Koban   1601; model for later koban
⑫Bunsei Nibukin   1818 ⑬Tenpo Nishukin   183
⑭Bunsei Isshukin 1824 ⑮Keicho Ichibukin   160
⑯Tenpo Ichibugin 1837 ⑰Meiwa Nishugin   177
⑱Kaei Isshugin   1854 ⑲Meiwa Gomonmegin   176

NAME	DATE ISSUED (A. D.)
①Wado Kaichin	708 Oldest silver coin
②Wado Kaichin	708 Oldest copper coin
③Kaiki Shoho	760 Oldest gold coin
④Jingo Kaiho	765
⑤Kaigen Tsuho	621 From China; model for later coinage
⑥Taikan Tsuho	1107 From China
⑦Eiraku Tsuho	15th C.; From China
⑧Kanei Tsuho	1636
⑨Tenpo Tsuho	1835
⑩Ibanashisen	1860 Directly from its cast

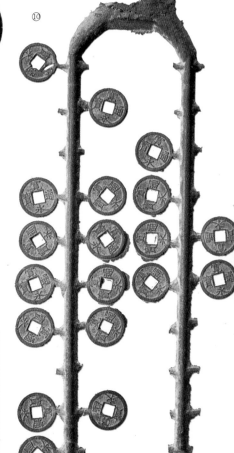

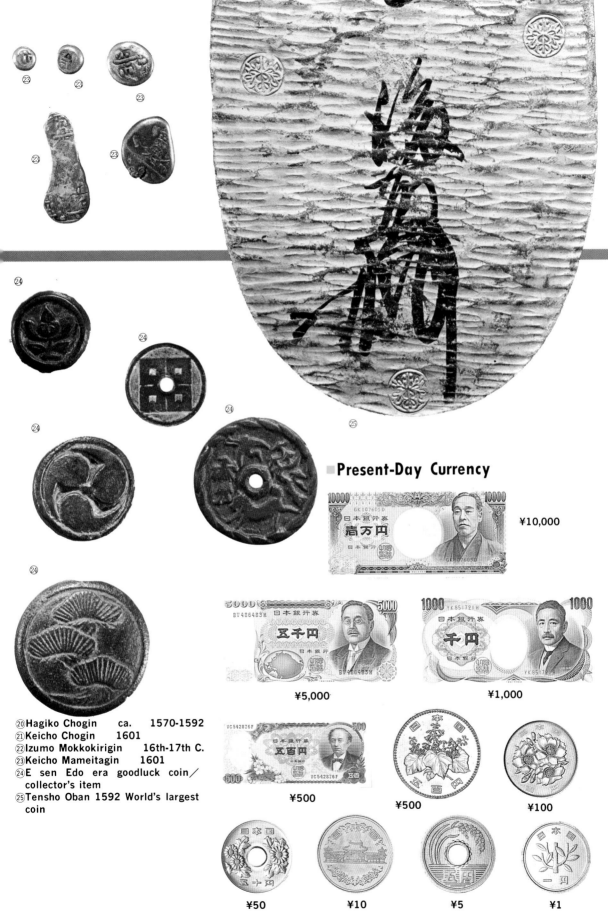

■Present-Day Currency

¥10,000

¥5,000

¥1,000

⑳Hagiko Chogin   ca.   1570-1592
㉑Keicho Chogin   1601
㉒Izumo Mokkokirigin   16th-17th C.
㉓Keicho Mameitagin   1601
㉔E sen Edo era goodluck coin／
   collector's item
㉕Tensho Oban 1592 World's largest
   coin

¥500

¥500

¥100

¥50

¥10

¥5

¥1

ENCOUNTERS WITH THE WEST

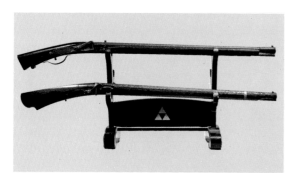

Muskets Called "Tanegashima arms" after the place of their introduction by the Portuguese. Domestic make (top). Portuguese make (bottom).

Musket Manual Marksmanship followed the introduction of muskets, and students received confidential manuals. (Inatomi School)

The European prominence began in the 16th century when a Chinese ship with Portuguese aboard shipwrecked at Tanegashima in southern Kyushu in 1543. The event had great impacts on Japan.

First, trade was started, for other Portuguese and succeeding Spanish ships anchored on Japan's coasts. Next, firearms were introduced.

Muskets brought by the Portuguese were welcomed as a new type of weapon which quickly spread among daimyo (feudal lords), and necessitated changes in warfare as well as castle construction. Finally, St. Francis Xavier made Christianity known in 1549. It spread rapidly. Some trade-minded daimyo protected its propagation while others, the so-called "Christian daimyo", even became converts.

New elements were thus added to the culture of Japan, though they did not necessarily survive intact. Indeed, Japan's 200 year policy of seclusion 90 years later so cut it off from the world that by the mid-17th century even the muskets were gone. A re-introduction of Western culture had to wait upon the forcible opening of the country in the latter half of the 19th century when Commodore Perry arrived.

St. Francis Xavier
"Temple" Interior Christian churches were referred to as "temples of the southern barbarians". They were built in Kyoto, Yamaguchi and elsewhere.

Folding Screen A number of pieces of *namban* (southern barbarian) art have survived and are valuable sources for historical research. Visible in the above painting are missionaries in clerical garb and black porters.

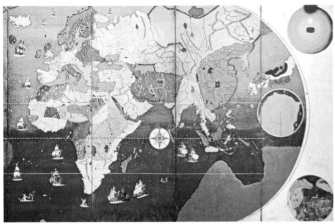

◀ **World Map** The fact that many folding screens like this were made attests to the heightened Japanese awareness and increased knowledge of lands abroad. Although copied and enlarged from a map obtained from a European, this screen is surprisingly accurate.

● EUROPEAN INFLUENCES

European culture brought many a change to Japanese life. One such was the performing of surgery at hospitals attached to the church. Furthermore, European printing presses were imported and books were printed in Roman letters.

◀ **Saddle inscribed with Roman letters**

▼ **Gunpowder container with Portuguese motif**

▲ *Tale of the Heike* in Roman letters

MISSION TO ROME

In 1582 three Christian daimyo (Otomo, Omura, Arima) under the urging of Fr. Valignano sent a mission of four young men to the Pope in Rome: Ito Mansho, Chijiwa Michael, Hara Martino, and Nakaura Julian, all 13-14 years old. They arrived in Rome three years and two months later to a tumultuous reception by the Pope and city. In 1590 they returned to Japan. The ruler at that time, Toyotomi Hideyoshi, summoned and had them perform some Western music for him, but since Christianity was by then proscribed, the four could not use the knowledge they'd gained abroad and led the remainder of their lives in obscurity.

THREE LEADERS OF THE SAMURAI

Feudatories waged fierce wars with one another from the late 1400s to the early 1600s, an epoch now known as the Era Of The Nation At War.

Because no one among the military was powerful enough to subdue the country for him, the emperor became but a symbol.

The incessant warfare of this epoch caused injustice to prevail; law and order decayed; the strong preyed upon the weak. Conversely, they were also vibrant times when abilities could be used to the fullest.

Order from the chaos was achieved by the power of three warriors: Oda Nobunaga, his vassal Toyotomi Hideyoshi, and his ally Tokugawa Ieyasu. They quelled the upheaval and made the country one.

The attributes these leaders displayed are highly admired by today's Japanese top management: Nobunaga was of stern temperament, but open to new ideas; Hideyoshi was well respected by his men as a student of human nature; Ieyasu was commedable for his long-suffering and endurance, regardless of the adversity.

▲Oda Nobunaga

▲Toyotomi Hideyoshi

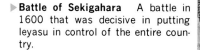

▶Battle of Sekigahara   A battle in 1600 that was decisive in putting Ieyasu in control of the entire country.

▲Ieyasu takes to the field astride his black mount.

▲**Battle of Nagashino**   Here in 1575 Nobunaga allied with Ieyasu to fight the Takeda army. The battle is famous for Nobunaga's clever use of matchlocks. Lining up his men in three ranks he had each row fire in turn, thus devastating the enemy.

▲**The Siege of Osaka**   Ieyasu slew Hideyoshi's son Hideyori when he attacked Osaka in 1615. This event broke the last resistance to the Tokugawa's, ended the age of war, and ushered in the era of the Tokugawa Shogunate.

OPULENT ART OF MOMOYAMA

In his later years, Hideyoshi built and lived in Fushimi Castle, Kyoto. This move inspired what later was called Momoyama culture. Its aura of grandeur and opulence reflected the tastes of the newly-risen daimyo who had succeeded to power as well as wealthy merchants.

Flowers, birds and even Chinese lions were painted in rich bold colors on goldleaf folding screens or heavy sliding panels to adorn castles or the homes of the military. Numerous screens depicted people enjoying such contemporary Japanese pastimes as shrine or temple observances, excursions to view the cherry blossoms or outings to enjoy the autumn leaves.

Distinctive to the arts of this era is their magnificent grandeur which sharply contrasts with the mental serenity so highly valued in Zen or Noh.

◄**Kodaiji** *Maki-e* The temple was erected in memory of Hideyoshi by his wife, Kita-no-Mandokoro. It is renowned for its *maki-e* (a design made by applying sprinkled powder of gold or silver to lacquer while it is still damp)

▼**Maple Panels** A classic example of large-paneled work on gold lacquer. The varied hues of autumn leaves are shown at their zenith, with emphasis on the maple.

Chinese Lions A folding screen attributed to Kano Eitoku and said to have belonged to Hideyoshi. Its opulent ethos is typical of Momoyama art.

Maple-viewing at Takao A forerunner of folding screens that depicted customs in vogue during the Momoyama era. Takao was (and is) a place near Kyoto noted for its fall leaves. Those who went to admire them included the military, the clergy and the townsfolk.

Early Kabuki Performance The first Kabuki was originated by women of easy virtue. One of the performers is shown wearing a crucifix.

CASTLES

Castles were originally strongholds against enemy invasion. Crude fortifications of stones piled one atop another on the slopes or tops of high hills were of course known from ancient times, but it was not until around the 15th century that the word *shiro* (castle) was brought into use.

In the 15th-16th centuries when internal warfare raged throughout the country, most castles were situated on hilltops for the obvious purpose of making attack difficult. After the 250 years of internal warfare were finally brought to an end, a major change in the nature of castles took place. Rather than being a place for waging war, they became a means of maintaining peace by securing themselves as administrative hubs which governed the people within their territories. Castles thus descended the mountains and became centers of communication which promoted castle towns.

The focal point of a Japanese castle is its *tenshukaku*, or what in the West would correspond to a keep. This towering, uppermost section of the castle was not only a symbol of the power of the daimyo who resided there but it also served as a symbol of the castle town. As such, it could be—and often was—artfully decorative. At present there are only 12 original *tenshukaku* remaining in Japan.

▼**Himeji Castle** Completed in 1610 when castle architecture was at its peak. Variations in the roof patterns create a beauty of their own.

▶**Matsumoto Castle** Built in the early 17th century. Its darkness makes it conspicuous against the whiteness of the snow. In the far distance are the Japan Alps.

TEA CEREMONY AND FLOWER ARRANGEMENT

The tea ceremony and flower arrangement, both influenced by Zen Buddhism, are classic examples of how everyday things in life can be elevated to an art. The tea ceremony, begun in the latter half of the 15th century, was perfected a century later by Sen no Rikyu, and today it is called *chado*. It is, simply put, no more than the making of *matcha* (powdered green tea) for a guest. It is, however, an artistic accomplishment that distills the beauty of life in its multi-faceted forms, and demands the utmost mental attitude and manners. The spirit underlying the tea ceremony is that of discovering beauty in the commonplace things of everyday life, taking the plain and simple as a principle.

Utter simplicity also governs the etiquette, utensils and décor.

Flower arrangement is another artistic accomplishment arising from daily life. It developed into an art form in the late 15th century. It is, on the surface, no more than simply arranging flowers attractively in a vase or other receptacle, as people anywhere in the world might do. However, to lovingly prolong the beauty of the fleeting life of a flower is also to bring about renewal in the heart of the arranger. Nature and the arranger thus become one, expressing therein a harmony between heaven, earth and humanity that is, in essence, the true art of flower arrangement (ikebana).

▲**Sen no Rikyu** The 16th-century perfecter of the tea ceremony, still regarded as the greatest of the tea masters.

▲*Akaraku* **Tea Bowl** One of the bowls favored by Sen no Rikyu. Like this one, tea bowls are simple but have something deep.

▲*Myokian-Taian* A tea hut built by Sen no Rikyu in southern Kyoto. Although the tea room is small (3.3m²), Rikyu enjoyed its rich spiritual atmosphere.

▲**Tea Ceremony** Detailed rules govern tea ceremony etiquette and movements. Depicted here is the return of the cup to the host after the guest has finished drinking.

▲**Tea Hut Exterior** Tea huts are usually made of plain wood. The path outside the entrance is laid with stepping stones. (Sankeien, Yokohama)

▶ **Tea Implements** A proper tea ceremony requires implements as these shown. Antique or hand-made utensils are treated like valuable objects of art.

◀**Flower Arrangement**
(above) Flowers arranged in the *tokonoma* (alcove) of a Japanese house. Arrangements for tea ceremonies are simple.
◀(below) Table piece for a Western-style house.

▲ **Flower Arrangement Students** Like the tea ceremony, flower arrangement is best done on *tatami* (mat) flooring. Nowadays it is often done while seated on a chair, and people abroad are showing increasing interest.

THE AGE OF THE SHOGUN

Tokugawa Ieyasu quelled the internal warfare, unified most of the country, and in 1603 became shogun, establishing his government in Edo (now Tokyo). This Edo-based shogunate lasted some 265 years and is called the Edo period.

Japan was divided into some 300 fiefs, each headed by a lord. These lords (daimyo) were required to live every other year in Edo. The idea was to force each daimyo to expend huge sums on travel and the maintenance of two estates so that he would be unable to accumulate the economic wherewithal to oppose the shogun. Wives and children always remained behind in Edo, much like hostages.

Since there were no major battles in this era, vassals could no longer demonstrate their loyalty to their lord under actual fighting conditions. To buttress the concept, a form of conduct arose whereby loyalty could be demonstrated. In extreme cases responsibility was assumed through hara-kiri if, for example, the lord died of illness or the vassal fell into disfavor. Such a moral code of loyalty and honor was called *bushido*. However, few samurai performed harakiri, and the shogunate soon issued a proclamation prohibiting it.

▼**Daimyo and Retinue**   On various occasions, especially on the way to or from a compulsory stay in Edo, the daimyo would form a huge procession of vassals to display his authority.

◄Yomei Gate at Nikko Shrine Ieyasu was enshrined in Nikko upon his death but the shrine itself was built in the time of his grandson Iemitsu (the third shogun). In the architecture of the gate the vestiges of the grandeur of Momoyama art are particularly evident.

►Martial Arts Warriors at outdoor practice. In the warless Edo period, stress was put on the cultivation of the mind and the attitude towards the sword and bow rather than on prowess in them.

▲Drawing of Edo Castle The original built by Ieyasu was destroyed in a fire. What remains is now part of the Imperial Palace.

THE CLOSING OF THE COUNTRY

The shogunate banned Christianity as being harmful to feudality while it simultaneously connived at its dissemination because it promoted trade. However, its suppression was later intensified and all missionary work forbidden when English and Dutch Protestants warned the government of the Spanish and Portuguese Catholics' territorial ambitions. In 1641 relations with all countries were cut off except for trade with Holland and China at Nagasaki. This reaction not only severed the influx of Christianity, but also gave the government a monopoly on trade. Japan incubated its indigenous life-style and culture in the succeeding 200 years of seclusion.

The 26 Martyrs Crucified in 1596, these converts and missionaries became the church's first martyrs in Japan. All were later elevated to sainthood by Rome.

(Above left) **Trading Ships (Shuinsen)** Such ships plied among the nations of S. E. Asia prior to the closure of the country.

(Above right) Japanese warrior, Hasekura Tsunenaga, baptized at Rome before the edict closing the nation.

The Shimabara Revolt Both the land and people of the Shimabara region were poor. The peasants sought salvation in Christianity, but the local lords suppressed it and imposed heavier taxes. In 1637 the peasants rioted, entrenched themselves in Hara Castle and inflicted heavy damage on the attacking armies.

▲**Virgin Mary** Believers who had only pretended to renounce Christianity made and worshipped statues of Mary in the likeness of Kannon, the Buddhist Goddess of Mercy, and were called "hidden Christians."

▶**Dejima** A tiny man-made islet in Nagasaki harbor where the Dutch conducted trade and from which they were forbidden to leave.

◀▶***Fumi-e* Plaque and Procedure** People had to tread on an image of Christ or Mary. To hesitate or refuse meant guilt.

▼**Trade at Dejima** All trade with Holland was conducted here.

▲**Temple Registry** Those whose names were unlisted were suspected of being Christians and arrested.

PEASANT-BASED WORK ETHIC

The Edo era's warrior class controlled the peasant class which constituted 80% of the population.

Peasants were harshly treated. Warriors demanded that 50% to 60% of their harvests be yielded as annual taxes. If one family in a group of five could not pay, the others had to balance the difference. This is a good example of the warrior class making use of the Japanese tendency toward groupism.

The government, for its part, directed detailed edicts at the peasants: "Divorce a luxury-loving wife, even if she be comely." "Rise early, work late." "Make simplicity your cloth."

High taxes and land rent forced the peasants to labor long and hard on small plots. Harvests were directly tied to how hard a person toiled, and most work was done by hand. Such a heritage has been a major source of Japanese industriousness.

● RICE-GROWING

▲**Transplanting** Seedlings are set out in the paddies, usually in June.

▲**Harvesting** A collective effort that begins in fall.

▲**Annual Taxes** Taxes levied on the village are carted off to storage.

▲**Farmhouse Interior** A well-to-do farmer's house of the early 18th century contained a hearth around which the family sat doing indoor chores.

▲**Peasants at Play** Harvest festivals provided one of the few non-working days available to peasants and were celebrated with much eating and drinking.

▲**Soup Line**   Peasants at the mercy of the weather were at times beset by misfortune. When there was no rice to eat, authorities made and distributed gruel.

▲**Farmhouse Yards**   Peasants labor in a Kyoto village.
◀**Rice Riot**   In times of poor harvests peasants demanded reductions in rice taxes; poor townspeople plundered rice shops in retaliation for exorbitant prices.

●EDUCATION FOR THE MASSES

There was no national educational system in the Edo era. However, various educational systems for commoners did exist. One such arrangement was the temple school. All over the country, teachers (priests, warriors, doctors) used temple facilities to teach groups of 20-30 students. The number of schools rose sharply around the mid-1700s. By the end of the era they reportedly reached some 15,000, a surprising figure when compared with today's 25,000 primary schools under the compulsory school system. Practical courses of reading, writing and calculation were taught.

For the children of the military class, there were schools on each fief. To develop the right mind-set, emphasis was initially put on the Chinese classics since their aim was to produce able administrators. Later, other subjects deemed useful to the clan were added: mathematics, medicine, Western studies, military science, etc. The shogunate had its own schools, which later formed the nucleus for Tokyo University.

▶(above) **Temple School**   Play-minded scholars have a lesson.
▶(below) **Clan School**   This one in Yamaguchi prefecture educated many of Japan's 19th century leaders.

A TALE OF THREE CITIES
(EDO, OSAKA, KYOTO)

Cities and castle towns were established nationwide from the latter half of the 16th century to the turn of the 17th. The three most populous—Edo, Osaka, Kyoto, known as "The Big Three"—were under the direct control of the government.

Edo, the government seat and political center, devoted some 60% of its area to districts for the warrior class. Hordes of merchants catered to their needs. By the 18th century, Edo's one million people made it the largest city in the world.

Osaka was the collection site for taxes and the clearinghouse for goods. It had a population of 350,000, an active money-lending business, and scores of business tycoons.

Kyoto had the court, a resplendent culture and approximately 400,000 people. It was the production center for high-grade weaving and crafts.

▲ **Nihonbashi in Edo** The first Shogun reclaimed this part of the coast and built this bridge. It marks the point from which all distances were measured.

▶ **Festival in Kanda** Dates from the Genroku era and is a source of pride for its inhabitants. Revelers carrying a portable shrine proceeded into the castle grounds for the Shogun's amusement.

▼ **Interior of Moneychanger's Shop** Eastern Japan centered on Edo and used gold. But western Japan centered on Osaka and used silver. Brokers facilitated currency exchanges. Also in use were copper coins of small denominations.

Trading Ship This type of ship ran along the coast between Edo and Osaka. Cargo consisted mainly of cotton, oil, vinegar and sake.

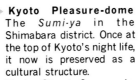

Messengers Hikyaku (runners) carried letters, documents and messages between distant places. The 560 km separating Edo and Osaka required one week.

Kyoto Pleasure-dome The *Sumi-ya* in the Shimabara district. Once at the top of Kyoto's night life, it now is preserved as a cultural structure.

Kyoto Street Scene Included are (right) a rich merchant's home, and (left) an umbrella maker's, a lacquerware shop and a writing-brush shop.

Osaka Waterfront The mouth of the Aji River was a busy terminus for the great shipping activity between Edo and Osaka.

GENROKU BOURGEOIS CULTURE

From the late 17th century to the turn of the 18th, the Japanese economy surged; and townsmen, in the course of spending their money, created a colorful culture called Genroku (1688-1703).

Such an affluent burgeois culture was a new, unique phenomenon. It flourished primarily among the middle-class of Kyoto, Osaka and its vicinities.

The common people now ventured into literature and art. There were writers like Ihara Saikaku, Matsuo Basho and Chikamatsu Monzaemon who gained popularity for portraying people realistically or writing boldly of love.

Art, too, brimmed with a sumptuousness that reflected the liberal spending power of the prosperous bourgeoisie.

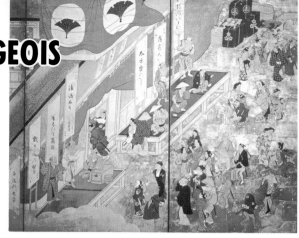

▲**Kabuki** An escalation in popularity in this era made it the top entertainment of the townspeople. Audiences ate and drank while enjoying the performances.

▲**Matsuo Basho** A grand master of *haiku* poetry who refined it to an art.
▲(right) **Ihara Saikaku** Wrote about money and sex.

▼**Katsura Rikyu (Detached Palace)** A pinnacle in Japan's landscape gardens. Built in 1620 for Emperor Goyozei's brother Prince Toshihito. Taut, a German architect, promoted its fame abroad after a 1933 visit.

▲*Mikaeri Bijin* By Moronobu. An original painting, not a *ukiyo-e* print.

▲**Irises** Decorative folding screens were greatly prized by prosperous merchants. Ogata Korin, the painter of this one, was born into the family of a well-to-do cloth merchant and is famous for his freshness of design.

◀**Wind Deity** Right side of a folding screen (left shows the deity of thunder) painted by Tawaraya Sotatsu. The grand scale probably appealed to the wealthy merchants.

●Genroku at a Glance

Genroku culture arose particularly from the lively enterprising towns-people of Kyoto and Osaka. Frugality conceded to an extravagance visible in every facet of their lives.

▼**Short-sleeved Kimono with Fall Flowers on White Cloth**

▶**Mt. Yoshino Painted on Tea Jar (Nonomura Ninsei)**
▼*Maki-e*-**style Writing Box with Arched Bridge (Honami Koetsu)**

▲**Decorative Comb**

▲▼**Hairpin**

KABUKI AND BUNRAKU

Noh, Kabuki and Bunraku are the major traditional performing arts. Noh developed in the latter half of the 14th century as entertainment for the shoguns and the military caste, whereas Kabuki and Bunraku developed from the 17th century as entertainment for the masses.

The essence of Kabuki can be found in the beauty of its traditional Japanese dancing. Accordingly, in its performance much stress is placed on stylized movements. Kabuki plays have a story, stage settings, musical accompaniment and dialog for the actors. The scenery and costumes, however, are eye-catchingly elaborate, and the actors' gestures and deliveries are highly exaggerated. As opposed to theater in the West, which is more or less grounded in realism, Kabuki tends to deal with the imaginary world. As in opera, Kabuki devotees enjoy the performance or interpretation of a particular actor in a particular role.

Perhaps Kabuki's greatest distinctness is its male enactment for both male and female roles. Kabuki was originally performed exclusively by females until allegations of morally disruptive behavior impelled an all-male cast.

Bunraku is a kind of puppet theater. A *tayu* (male reciter) is seated on a revolving dais next to the puppets' stage. A *shamisen* player sits by him. The tayu chants the narration and all the puppets' lines as the shamisen is played. Stories and plots mainly treat such themes as the love-vs.-duty conflicts that arise from the contradictions inherent in a feudal society. The movements of the dolls are synchronized with the melodious, deep-toned strumming of the shamisen and reciting. The dolls, about one meter (3 feet) tall, require three operators each. The first manipulates the head and right arm; the second operates the left arm, and the third operator manipulates the legs and feet. Although incapable of altering their facial expressions, the dolls are so skillfully manipulated to express emotions ranging from grief to laughter that they seem to be imbued with the very breath of life, much to the delight of the audience.

▲**Stage with *Hanamichi*** A raised runway that cuts through the audience on the left to join the stage at a right angle. It heightens the sense of audience participation.

◄**Kabuki Makeup** The actor's face is made up with *kumadori* paint to highlight the character, in this case the violent and powerful nature of a demon.

▲ **Oyama** Kabuki is performed entirely by male actors. Those who play female roles are called *oyama*, and outdo women in expressing stylized concepts of femininity.

▲ **Striking a Pose** At a peak moment in a performance an actor will strike an exaggerated pose (*mie*). This brings on audience applause and the yelling out of the actor's stage name by aficionados.

▲ **Stage Properties** The Kabuki stage uses a variety of props. The huge toad would certainly be a surprise to any first-timer.

▲ **Bunraku Doll** A scene from Chikamatsu's Joruri, *The Love Suicide at Sonezaki*. The dolls express such subtle emotions that they seem imbued with life.

▼ **Tayu** and **Shamisen** **Player** The *tayu* narrates the story; the player provides the musical accompaniment. Both are to stage left.

▲ **Dolls and Operators** One doll requires three operators. The assistant operators wear black masks, but the chief operator is sometimes bare-faced.

MARTIAL ARTS AND SUMO

The strategy in combative sports in Japan is to passively take advantage of an opponent's power by making it work against him.

The principal technique of the martial arts is that of pulling: the tugging of one's opponent in judo, the pulling motion on the sword in kendo, the pulling actions in karate, etc. It is supposedly the same motion used when tilling a field with a hoe. It is also contrary to the Western approach of charging aggressively forward: the lancing of the sword in fencing, the thrusting of the fists in boxing, etc. The latter motion is used by men and animals when they fight.

Judo, kendo, archery, karate and other Japanese martial arts were originally to protect oneself from personal attack. Later they developed into disciplines of the mind and body under the influences of Buddhism and Confucianism. These martial arts thus possess both a physical, practical aspect —the techniques and methods of defense —and a spiritual aspect—ethics and morals. As in all sports, martial arts teach the meaning and importance of fair play, loyalty, and honor. They have now come to be enjoyed like most other sports.

Japan's national and most popular sport is sumo. In olden times, sumo was associated with the art of divination; the winner's village was supposedly favored with a good harvest.

Nowadays, sumo is a sport only. Over the past two decades a handful of foreign participants have climbed into the sumo ring, and Akebono, a native of Hawaii, attained the highest rank in sumo, and became the first foreign yokozuna.

▲**Sumo Arena**   A display of wrestlers gets underway in the ring prior to the day's bouts at Tokyo's Sumo Wrestling Amphitheater. 15-day tournaments are held six times a year.

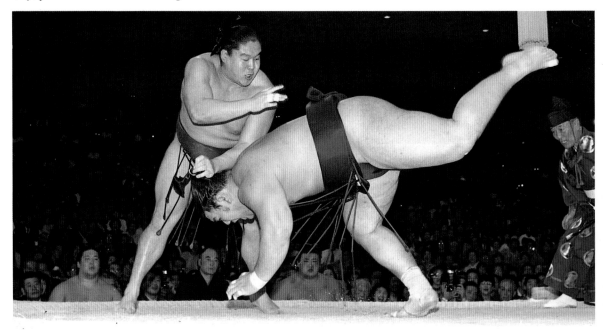

▲**Sumo Match**   Two wrestlers vie in each bout. The loser is the one pushed out first or who touches any part of the ring with any part of his body other than the soles of his feet.

72

▲**Kyudo** The archer learns to respect and understand his limitations and potentials.

▷**Kendo** Kendo is taught as a sport at junior and senior high schools to instill self-discipline.

▲**Karate** A combative technique that uses no weapons. It is generally believed to have originated in Tang China, but some theories favor Korea or even Okinawa.

◁**Judo** Judo is another form of unarmed combat, differing from karate in that it employs throws and holds whereas karate uses hands and feet. Judo originated in Japan, but is now a worldwide sport. Since the 1964 Tokyo Olympics it has been a regular Olympic event.

KASEI CULTURE AND UKIYO-E

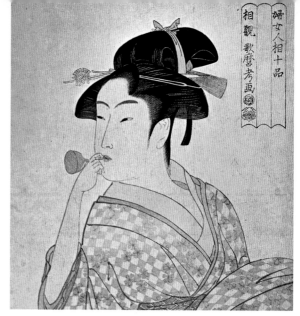

From the mid-1700s to the beginning of the 1800s, the economic center of the Edo era gradually shifted from the Kyoto-Osaka area to Edo. The cultural capital accordingly re-established in Edo. This relocation marked a new cultural era called Kasei, for it combines two eras that comprise it: Bun*ka* (1804-1817) and Bun*sei* (1818-1829).

Kasei culture penetrated beyond the prosperous middle classes of the Genroku era to the lower classes. Books therefore began employing simple sentences written in the vernacular; they were illustrated and frequently focused on humorous themes.

Ukiyo-e prints became popular and expanded beyond images of actors and beautiful women to include landscapes. It is from this period that much of popular culture springs.

▲**Woman with Glass Toy** By Kitagawa Utamaro, famous for his prints of beautiful women. Early ukiyo-e prints were done in one color or two but by this period many colors were used.

▶**Akasaka Stage of the Tokaido** The artist, Ando Hiroshige, was the foremost portrayer in ukiyo-e of Japanese-style landscapes.

▼**The 47 Samurai** The story of a lord whose conduct brings on his forced suicide (*harakiri*). Later, his vassals slay the instigators. This 1702 event was performed as a kabuki play in 1748 and remains a favorite tragedy since it appeals to the sympathy traditionally shown to unfairly treated people who die tragic deaths.

▲**Electric Generator** Hiraga Gennai, an inventor, repaired this generator obtained from a Hollander and succeeded in making it work. A budding scientific spirit was astir in the era.

▲**Actor** In bold strokes, Sharaku captured an actor's personality.

▶ **Wave at Kanagawa** Hokusai's originality of expression influenced even the French impressionists.

◀ **Ryogoku Area** Aodo Denzen studied Western art and became proficient in the depiction of perspective.

▶ **Hippocrates** "The Father of Medicine" by Watanabe Kazan, a student of Dutch learning.

●Personal Possessions of the Townspeople

People in the Edo era owned things of a rather extravagant nature. Made by the hands of expert craftsmen they are precious in contrast to the mass-produced items of today.

▲ *Inro* A pill box worn at the sash.

▶ **Lantern** Thin paper outside, a candle within.

◀ **Tooth Blackener** In the Edo era, wives commonly blackened their teeth.

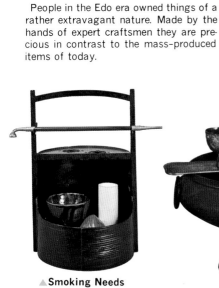

▲**Smoking Needs**

JAPANESE GARDENS

The Japanese have a great fondness for gardens, stemming perhaps from a sense of having lived in harmony with nature for so long. They tend to fill any open spaces on their plots with trees or plants no matter how small these spaces may be. At the same time as the Japanese seek the quiet repose of nature in a garden, they also try to create there a kind of universe in miniature. This practice goes as far back as the Heian era when nobles incorporated into their gardens the imagery of a perfect world (paradise). Later, in the Kamakura and Muromachi eras, Zen priests created rock gardens in which stones were likened to mountains or Buddhist images, sand to oceans, and so on.

There are of course many gardens enjoyed solely for their natural beauty. In the Edo era (1603-1868) feudal lords often built huge rambling gardens for strolling in, some of which survive today in the form of public or private parks.

Garden construction reflects the Japanese ideal of beauty. Japanese gardens differ from Western gardens in that the former, instead of symmetrical, orderly arrangements, prefer more abstract, natural ones that display nature's many facets as they are, emphasizing unbalanced gracefulness.

▶**Kenrokuen**   Used to be the garden of Lord Maeda, whose fief in Kaga yielded the largest amount of harvest excluding that of the Tokugawa shoguns. From the early 17th century to the early 19th, repeated expansion and restoration made the garden what it is today. It is an excellent example of the strolling-type of garden. The pond in the center and the stone lantern nearby present a scene of beautiful harmony in their covering of snow. (Kanazawa, Ishikawa pref.)

▲**Ritsurin Park**   Formerly the garden of Lord Matsudaira, ruler of the province of Takamatsu in Shikoku. Clusters of stones form islands in the six ponds spanned by gracefully curved wooden bridges. (Takamatsu, Kagawa pref.)

▲**Shugakuin Detached Palace Garden**   Built in the late 17th century for Emperor Gomizunoo at his Kyoto villa. Incorporates court refinement.

▲**Zuisenji Garden**   The original, built in the middle of the 14th century, was long neglected until restored in 1970. The pond was created by excavating the foot of a hillside. (Kamakura, Kanagawa pref.)

▼ **Daisenin Garden** A mid-16th century Zen garden in Kyoto, part of the one on p. 45 lower right. White sand represents a large river and two islands.

▶ **Korakuen** Once the garden of Lord Ikeda who ruled the Okayama fief. Completed in 1701, it is one of Japan's top three gardens.

TRADITIONAL HOUSES

A traditional Japanese house is made of wood and paper, and provides good ventilation. The essential structure is of wood.

The sliding partitions are called either *fusuma* (a solid paper partition on a wooden frame), or *shoji* (a paper-windowed partition on a wooden frame). They are miscalled "doors" by Westerners; actually, they are a kind of room divider.

Susceptibility to fire is a drawback for such houses, but their suitability to Japan's humid summers and their resiliency to earthquakes are definite advantages. The fact that the Horyuji, a 7th-century wood structure, is still standing, says much for the excellence of wood as a building material.

The biggest difference between Western and Japanese houses is probably in the concept of rooms. In Japan, rooms are divided by the afore-mentioned *shoji* and *fusuma* and have no locks. Also, each room can function as living room, dining room, or bedroom, and removing the *shoji* or *fusuma* partitions results in one big room. In comparison with a Western house, where each room is independent and has but one function, the Japanese house is multi-functional in construction and highly versatile. The adaptability of a Japanese house likely accounts for the West's misconception that a Japanese cannot maintain any privacy at home and is afforded little personal independence.

In the past few decades, houses built of concrete have increased in number, but the touch of wood is something the Japanese are unwilling to forsake. Most of the interiors of concrete houses are consequently of wood, even if it is only wood paneling.

▲**Former Nara Family Home**　Built in the latter half of the 18th century. The roof, as befits a house in a farming village, is thatched, but spectacularly so. A rich farmer's house of the first rank in the northeast. (Akita prefecture)

▲**Nara Home Interior**　The special parlor where relatives gathered at such times as New Year's to exchange formalities with the family head. *Shoji* to the left, *fusuma* to the right, *irori* (a hearth) is in the center. *Tatami* flooring is unusual for a room with *irori*.

▲**The Osumi Home**   Late 17th-century home of upper-class merchant built along a main road in Shiga prefecture. It served as both a pharmacy and a lodging house for daimyo. The woodwork under the eaves is especially noteworthy.

▲**The Kometani Home**   A mid-18th century merchant's home in Imai, Nara prefecture. The walls were stuccoed and windows kept few as a precaution against fire. Imai is a famous town of old merchant homes.

▶**The Toyoda Home**   Merchant's house built in the latter half of the 17th century. A big crest of a tree adorns this home of Edo era lumber dealers. The second-story lattice-work is decorative. (Imai)

▼**The Sasagawa Home**   The family, major landowners in the Niigata plains and the Edo era's major rice producers, also served as village officials. They thus adopted features of military-class homes such as the entryway construction to the left.

MODERNIZATION-CUM-WESTERNIZATION

Despite its massive importation of Chinese culture in earlier epochs, Japan never lost its Japaneseness. What was imported was not always adopted, and what was adopted was nearly always adapted or Japanized to suit Japanese life. Continental culture was considered important but not the absolute standard.

Accordingly, in the 19th century when Western imperialism was on the march and came knocking on Japan's gates in the form of Commodore Perry in 1853, Japan had only to look at China being carved up by the Western powers to realize that the only way to save itself from the same fate would be to end its 200-year policy of seclusion, open its doors to the West, and again import, evaluate and adapt. The process, however, was often limited to the outward forms and manifestations of Western civilization rather than its spirit which, being based on a long tradition of Christianity, was unsuitable for the Japanese to absorb.

▲**Rokumeikan Ball**   To show the West that Japan was equally modern, the government constructed this building to hold balls to which the entire diplomatic corps was invited.

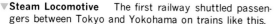

▼**Steam Locomotive**   The first railway shuttled passengers between Tokyo and Yokohama on trains like this.

▶**Rickshaws** Made in the late 19th century, they soon became popular.

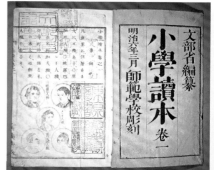

▶ **1870 s Primer**

●Objects of Interest

Interest in things foreign ranged from items of daily use to Western-style clothes.

▲ **Brick Building** Few remain in today's Tokyo.

◀ **Barber shop** To abandon the traditional topknot for a Western-style cut was a mark of a cultured man.

▲ **Stein**

◀ **Mantle Clock**

▲ **Lamp**

THE DAWN OF MODERN CULTURE

Japan's Westernization was too rapid to be anything but superficial. Old temples were suddenly considered worthless; pagodas that today are national treasures stood in danger of being torn down; ukiyo-e prints, looked upon as mere craftwork, were disposed of like so much wastepaper. Indeed, the first to recognize their value and preserve them were the art historians of the West.

A counterreaction against this rapid Westernization set in around 1887. It was not so radical as to draw the nation back into its isolationist shell, for the Japanese appreciated Western civilization's strengths. It was instead a stabilizing period Japan needed in order to harmonize the Japanization of Western adaptations with existing Japanese traditions. The fusion of the two created a new modern culture.

Western techniques in art, for example, were applied to Japanese themes; Western music was introduced into school curriculums, and similar advances were made in the natural sciences.

▲ *MUGA* (selflessness), by Yokoyama Taikan

▲ *ROEN* (old monkey), by Takamura Koun, who created modern, realistic works using Japanese techniques of wood carving.
◀ *HIBO KANNON* (Merciful Mother) by Kano Hogai

▲*BUGI*(Dancing Girl) by Kuroda Seiki
◀*"Japanese* Woman" by Ragusa*, an Italian sculptor invited to Japan to teach at a college of fine arts.

◀**Meiji Era** Japan's Westernization occured mainly in the large cities. Elsewhere, basically little changed from the previous era except perhaps hairstyles.

●WESTERN STYLE ARCHITECTURE

Western architectural concepts were rapidly introduced. Though initial results were an irregular intermingling when blended with Japanese architecture, full mastery was eventually achieved with the help of foreign technicians.

▲**Residence of Saigo Tsugumichi**

▲**Former Akasaka Detached Palace** Now used as a state guest house.

THE PACIFIC WAR AND ASIANISM

Following the opening of the country, top priority was given to strengthening the nation, and European systems were enthusiastically incorporated to that effect; thus Japan became the first Asian nation with a modern constitution and parliament.

But this governmental achievement encouraged unfavorable actions. Japan's successes emboldened it to invade a weakened China in the 1920s. Japan thereafter believed its destiny was to liberate Asia from the yoke of Western imperialism, so set out to dominate Asia under the motto "Asia for the Asiatics". This led to the Pacific War in December, 1941. By this time the Japanese were unable to stop the rampant militarism of its war machine, and paid for that inability in the atomic bombing.

Japan rid itself of every vestige of ultranationalism after its defeat. It started afresh as a democratic state, constructing a cultural and economically-based nation.

▲The rising sun flag floating high in Singapore

▲**Tokyo in Ashes** Repeated bombings, especially the major one in March, 1945, left Tokyo in ruins.

▲**Wartime Citizens of Tokyo** Aerial bombings were intensified from the end of 1944 and air-raid drills became more frequent.

▼**Wartime Civilian Garb** Steel helmet on the back was worn during air raids.

▲**Women's Wartime Wear** Baggy pants (monpe) were worn instead of banned skirts. The hood was for air raids.

A Practical Guide to
THE LIVING TRADITIONS OF JAPAN

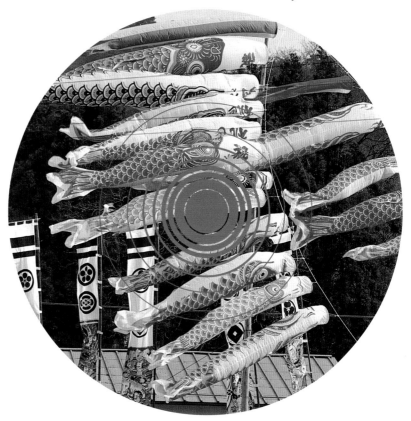

JAPANESE RITES OF PASSAGE

The hope of having a healthy and happy life is a universal one that remains unchanged from ancient times.

Upon reaching each of life's milestones, the Japanese give thanks for arriving thus far and ask for future blessings through prayer. The most numerous rites of passage are those arising from the wish of parents for the healthy growth of their children.

The figures for life span during the 1890s were 42.8 years for men and 44.3 years for women; the infant mortality rate was high. Therefore it is not surprising that so many celebrations exist for a child's safe transition from one stage of life to another. Japan's most colorful ritual is the wedding ceremony. Customs differed from locality to locality until about 200 years ago, but presently either Buddhist, Shintoist, or Christian weddings are performed. Common rituals throughout the country are given here.

▲**First Shrine Visit**   Boys are taken 30 days after birth, girls 31. As a rule the mother's family provides the finery, and the paternal grandmother carries the baby.

▲**Shichi-Go-San (7-5-3 Festival)**   Girls three and seven, and boys five, dress up in new outfits on November 15th and visit shrines to pray for their safe and healthy future.

▲**Starting School**   The school year begins in April. Parents usually accompany their children to the entrance ceremony.

▲**Coming-of-Age Day**   On January 15th, a national holiday, those who have attained the age of 20 are recognized as adults. Towns and villages sponsor various events.

Wedding Ceremony A peak among life's many rites of passage. The average age for the groom is 27, for the bride 23. Most weddings are conducted according to Shinto rites, but there are also Buddhist and Christian services. There are some 730,000 weddings each year and 180,000 divorces.

Wedding Reception The actual wedding is witnessed only by the go-betweens and the parents and relatives of the bride and groom. The reception that immediately follows is attended by the above and invited guests and lasts two to three hours.

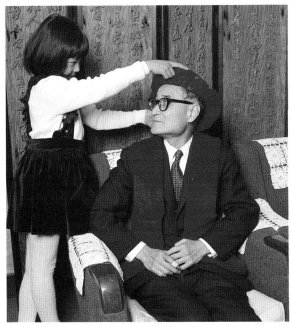

Kanreki A celebration for those who attain their 61st calendar year. It marks the completion of one full cycle of the Ten Calendar Signs and the Twelve Zodiacal Signs so that a person figuratively enters a "second childhood". To celebrate, a red cap and vest (chanchanko) are worn.

Funeral Weddings mainly follow Shinto rites, but funerals are mostly conducted according to Buddhist ritual. Only 10% are performed along Christian or Shinto lines. Undertakers handle arrangements, and Buddhist priests conduct religious services.

ANNUAL EVENTS

The fact that the Japanese are able to keep alive so many traditions is due in good part to the various celebrations that take place throughout the year. One such observance—the year's biggest—is New Year's, which lasts from January 1st to 3rd.

Preparations start getting underway toward the close of the old year. Government offices, private businesses and industries begin closing down around the 29th of December. There then follows a mass exodus from the cities as people stream back to their home towns, overloading every available means of transportation in the process. Meanwhile, homes are thoroughly cleaned inside and out so that the New Year will get off to a fresh start; pine branches are arranged at the front gate or door, sacred straw festoon are hung, and traditional foods to be eaten during the holidays are prepared. On New Year's Eve, many families sit down to a bowlful of a long, slender-type of noodle as a symbolic wish for a long life.

At midnight, temples throughout the nation slowly ring their bells 108 times in order to expiate what Buddhism considers the 108 inherent evil desires one must rid oneself of to live a wholesome life. Many people go to temples or shrines on the following days to pray for health and prosperity.

At home they enjoy traditional foods (*ozoni*) and amuse themselves with one or another of the many New Year's games. Children, meanwhile, receive gifts of money called *otoshi-dama* in traditional envelopes from family and relatives.

▲*Kadomatsu* These decorations of pine and bamboo adorn both sides of entryways at New Year's. Pine and bamboo symbolize longevity.

▲**Battledore** Decorated paddles keep aloft a shuttlecock with a tiny bell affixed to it. A classical New Year's game for girls that is gradually disappearing.

▲**First Prayer** People go to shrines to pray for a good year. Some buy paper fortunes there, as these young ladies have done.

Kite-flying Flying kites used to be a popular activity for boys at New Year's. However, the decrease in open areas and the proliferation of telephone lines have placed this traditional pastime in danger of disappearing.

Kaki-zome The year's first formal writing with a brush, usually on January 2nd. Students are often assigned this as homework to improve their writing. Here it is done at a shrine, though home is the usual place.

●KARUTA AND HYAKU-NIN-ISSHU

Karuta and *Hyaku-nin-isshu* are typical indoor games enjoyed during the New Year holidays. *Karuta* takes its name from a game introduced from Portugal in the 16th century. The game itself has since become thoroughly Japanese. It is played with a deck of 100 cards divided into 50 with pictures and 50 with short phrases or proverbs on them. The picture cards visually depict the ideas expressed on the word cards, and are laid out faceup on the playing surface in random order. From the stack of 50 word cards a reader draws and reads aloud one card. The other players then vie to see who can first take up the picture card that corresponds to the verse. The person with the most cards at the end of the game is the winner.

Hyaku-nin-isshu is similar to *karuta*. On the cards, however, are poems by famous poets from the 7th to the 13th centuries. Word cards have the entire poem plus a likeness of the poet. The matching cards bear only the concluding verse. When the reader begins to read out the first lines of the poem, the players recalling the ending verse try to be the first to locate and take that card.

In the eras when the 100 poets were active it was conventional for the nobility and upper classes to quote poetry in their conversations and correspondence. Skill at this for both men and women was a barometer of how cultured they were. A more suitable game to evoke the elegant atmosphere of those bygone days would be hard to find. Some of the card sets are beautiful enough to be called works of art.

Hyaku-nin-isshu Cards Each card has on it a poem from ancient times and a likeness of the poet.

▶**Hyaku-nin-isshu game** As shown by these players in old court attire, this play-at-home game is also enjoyed at shrines during New Year's.

Many events take place throughout the year. Some are celebrations that now occur only in limited regions, although the ones given here are common events observed nationwide.

One celebration that probably differs from those abroad is *Kodomo-no-Hi*, Children's Day (May 5th). Originally an old traditional ceremony to mark the growth of a son, May 5th was not officially designated a national holiday until after the Second World War. The fact that a day exists solely for children suggests the degree to which family life in Japan is child-centered, as opposed to the more adult-centered family in the West. Other red-letter days include Mother's Day (the second Sunday in May) and Father's Day (the 3rd Sunday in June.)

▲**Setsubun**   The day before the first day of spring (by the old calendar), either the 3rd or 4th of February. People throw parched beans within the home to drive demons out and bring good fortune in. The day is also observed at temples and shrines.

▼*Hina-Matsuri* **(Doll Festival)**   A March 3rd fete to wish girls happiness. Court dolls are displayed at home and special food is eaten. Peach trees are in bloom at this time, so it is also called "Peach Festival".

Flower Festival April 8th, Buddha's birthday. Temples observe a ritual in which sweet tea (symbolizing the birth bath) is poured over small statues of Buddha.

Boy's Festival May 5th has long been the day for boys. Military dolls are displayed so that boys will grow up to possess the Japanese ideals of manhood.

▼*Hana-mi* From late March to early April the cherry blossoms bloom and people hold parties with picnics and merrymaking beneath the boughs at night as well as in the daytime to welcome the coming of spring.

▲*Koi-Nobori* **(Carp Streamers)** These cloth streamers, flown on and around May 5th, express the hope that sons will be as vigorously healthy as the carp that swim against the stream. May 5th is also called Kodomo-no-Hi (Children's Day) because it is now celebrated for girls as well.

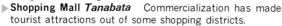

▲**Tanabata** A July 7th star festival, Chinese in origin, to celebrate the annual tryst of Altair and Vega, stars separated by the Milky Way. People decorate bamboo branches with paper ornaments and prayer cards, and place them in the garden or hang them from eaves.

▶**Shopping Mall** *Tanabata* Commercialization has made tourist attractions out of some shopping districts.

▲**Fireworks Display** Fireworks extravaganzas are held in most localities on July and August nights.

▲**Bon Odori** The week around July 15th (August 15th in some areas) is called *o-bon*, a time for consoling the spirits of the dead. Neighborhood groups gather for dancing (*odori*) to the music of flutes and drums.

▲**Cemetery Visits** The spring and fall equinoxes are times for remembering ancestors. Because of such religious awareness, the Japanese faith is sometimes referred to as "ancestor worship".

◀**Maple Viewing** Autumn's counterpart to spring's cherry-blossom viewing. The custom is especially noticeable in Kyoto, where there are many places renowned for autumn maple leaves.

▼(lower left) **Chrysanthemum Dolls** Mums are about as Japanese as cherry blossoms. Dolls crafted from them are a common sight in fall. Themes are often taken from Kabuki.

▼(lower right) **Battledore Fair** At the end of December, fairs selling New Year goods are held at shrines. Paddles sold are often for decoration, not actual use.

THE IMPERIAL INSTITUTION

Except for the period of national consolidation from the 4th through the 7th centuries, the emperors of Japan have almost never held political power and therefore have rarely been directly involved in political strife. This peaceful image and the aura of historical tradition and sanctity surrounding him have firmly embedded the concept of the emperor as the focus of unity in the minds of the Japanese people.

Under state-fostered Shinto from the time of the Showa Emperor's grandfather, and in the period prior to World War II when ultranationalistic thought swept Japan, the Emperor was called a "living man-god" and the nation treated as one family with the Emperor at its head. In 1946, however, the Showa Emperor renounced this mystique of divinity, and under the present constitution has become a symbol of the unity of the people.

From the historical perspective, the imperial institution has been maintained through the hereditary transmission of religious authority. Festivals and rites for bountiful harvests were ritualized and institutionalized, always with the emperors acting as high priests. The system thus had its beginnings with the emperor acting as the head of a primitive state in which his prayers determined courses of action. Vestiges of this role can still be seen today in the ceremonial transplanting and harvesting of rice that the Emperor performs within the palace grounds each year.

The personal name of the Showa Emperor is Hirohito. His ascension to the throne took place in 1926, which made him the longest-reigning emperor in the nation's history.

The demise of emperor Hirohito in 1989 marks the end of the longest imperial reign in Japanese history. The new emperor, Akihito, is the 125th in the imperial line.

The new empress, Michiko, who is not of imperial birth, married Akihito in April, 1959.

◀The Emperor and Empress visiting a health clinic for mothers and children The imperial couple take delight in the welcome of the children. In the background is a collage of the seabed the children have made.

▼The new Emperor carrying out his official duties The new Emperor has declared to the nation that he will promote pacifism on the basis of the Japanese Constitution.

▲ **The Imperial Family** Taken on Dec 23, 1993, the Emperor's Birthday.

▼ **The Crown Prince and Princess** In January 1993, Crown Prince Naruhito married Masako Owada, a Harvard- and Oxford-educated diplomat.

▲ **Visiting a Home for the Elderly** The present Emperor and Empress are here accompanied by their youngest daughter, Nori-no-miya.

▲ **Hiro-no-miya Inspecting a TV Studio** The youthfulness and unreserved manner of the Crown Prince have won him the affection of the Japanese people.

TRADITIONAL JAPANESE COOKING

When we examine the dietary life of the modern Japanese, we find an enormous diversity, with traditional Japanese cooking existing side by side with, and sometimes incorporating, cooking from around the world adapted to the Japanese taste. The gustatory preferences of the Japanese have clearly changed. Nevertheless, the special form and spirit of traditional cooking and dietary life remain deep-rooted.

We can distinguish three main features in traditional cooking. Firstly, premium is placed upon freshness and innate flavor, which are brought out to the full in the cooking. Secondly, the Japanese aesthetic sense is displayed in the arrangement of the food and in the choice of receptacles for serving it. A sense of season, a feeling for nature, and an eye for color are skilfully incorporated. Thirdly, Japanese cooking derives from a non-meat eating culture. The staple food is rice, with fish and vegetables forming the nucleus of the side dishes.

These features together form a harmonious whole and have made Japanese cooking what it is.

▲A splendid harmony between the simplicity of the herring and the brilliant yellow of the dish.

▲An elegant combination of the red, yellow, green, brown, and white of the food in a bowl suggesting the sun and the moon.

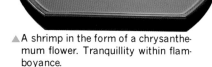
▲A shrimp in the form of a chrysanthemum flower. Tranquillity within flamboyance.

◀Cool and refreshing food in a clear dish. A masterly suggestion of summer.

A Historical Look at Japanese Cooking
●Shojin ryori (vegetarian cooking)

The Zen sect of Buddhism was spread in Japan from around the beginning of the 13th century by the efforts of two monks, Eisai (1141-1215) and Dogen (1200-1253), and a large number of Zen temples were built. The daily diet in these temples was vegetarian, and with the popularization of the Zen sect, *shojin ryori* (vegetarian cooking) permeated the eating habits of the people at large, partly because it was served at Buddhist memorial services.

Buddhist influence in Japan from early on had established the custom that meat was not generally eaten. *Shojin ryori* went to the logical extreme, derived as it was from Buddhist bans on the killing of living things and the consumption of alcohol. It became a virtue to be satisfied with simple, even coarse, food.

In *shojin ryori* vegetable protein, oils and fats are skilfully incorporated so that even from the point of view of modern dietetics, it provides a healthy well-balanced diet.

●Receptacles and the Arrangement of Food

It has often been said that Japanese cooking is "a feast for the eyes." It is to that extent that great care is taken in the choice of bowls and dishes, and the arrangement of food, as well as in the beauty of the food itself.

Dishes and bowls, in their color, shape and texture, should harmonize with, and enhance, the cooking. The food should look refined as well as delicious so that the color and shape of the bowls in which it is served must also be refined. The arrangement of the food takes into account both the season, and the harmony and balance of the food with the dishes to be used. A sense of space and suggestiveness should pervade the clearly-defined arrangement.

▲ Elegant pale blue porcelain contrasting with the bright red and white. An impression of balance between movement and stillness.

▲ The red maple is redolent of the quiet deep in the mountains, and the food suggests the autumn harvest.

◀ Ordinary ingredients go into making this food, served in an ornate dish decorated with gold and flowers. The greenery on top is also striking.

▶ The gold and the butter, and the celadon and the green pepper set each other off to perfection, engendering a strange charm.

▲ Fois gras bean curd (*tofu*) with a round Japanese fan beneath the plate. A splendid meeting between East and West.

●Honzen ryori (formal banquet-style cooking)

Cooking developed into an art in the 14th century. It was a time when there was much interaction between the court aristocracy and the new warrior ruling class. The code of manners for the warriors was strictly enforced, and even the way food was to be prepared for, and served to, guests was laid down both in form and content.

The refined cuisine which developed out of the formal styles of those times was developed further in the Edo period (1603-1868) as *honzen ryori* (literally, "main table") by the high-class restaurants of the time. *Honzen ryori* is the basis of Japanese cooking in form and etiquette.

Honzen ryori is served on small low individual tables called *zen* which look like four-legged trays. The tables are named for the order in which they appear: *honzen* (main table), *ni no zen* (second table), *san no zen* (third table), and so on. A completely separate table called the *suimono zen* is used for serving *sake*.

●AN OUTLINE OF JAPANESE COOKING

Here we shall mention some of the types of Japanese cooking that are popular both within and without Japan. They are all integral components of modern cuisine, old and familiar dishes well-loved by the Japanese, and each exhibits the characteristics of Japanese cooking.

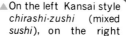

▲On the left Kansai style *chirashi-zushi* (mixed *sushi*), on the right Tokyo style *nigiri-zushi* (hand-formed *sushi*). The distinctive harmony between the fish and the vinegared rice is a typically Japanese taste.

▲**Sashimi** Fresh, uncooked seafood. The taste varies with the skill with which the knife is used in cutting the fish. Here, *fugu-sashi* (balloon fish sashimi) is arranged on a large plate in the shape of a chrysanthemum.

◀**Tempura** Its origins reputed to stem from the Portuguese cooking introduced in the 17th century, *tempura* is deep-fried fresh seafood and vegetables. One of the favorite Japanese foods abroad.

●Chakaiseki (tea ceremony cuisine)

The tea ceremony was formalized by Sen no Rikyu (1522-1591) in the latter half of the 16th century. *Chakaiseki* is the food served before the powdered green tea (*matcha*) appears during the tea ceremony. It is plain and simple, just enough to help an empty stomach endure.

Originally it was the custom that the person who gave the tea ceremony also prepared the food himself. However, by the middle of the 19th century special shops catering for the tea ceremony had made their appearance, and today in most cases it is such specialists who continue to exercise their talent. In the circumstances, the simple *chakaiseki*, which at first consisted only of one soup and two or three side dishes, gradually became more lavish.

Today, the standard menu has become two dishes added to the basic one soup and three side dishes. A further two or three dishes, such as a soy-flavored or a vinegared dish, may be added.

▶ **Sukiyaki** A dish special to Japan comprising meat, vegetables, bean curd, etc. simmered in a sauce of which soy sauce and sugar are the main ingredients. *Sukiyaki* is representative of the many varieties of one-pot table cooking (*nabemono*) and is famous the world over.

▶ **Two Dishes Made from Bean Curd (tofu)** In recent years bean curd has been gaining attention abroad as a health food. Its attraction is its lightness and simplicity, together with its rich and nourishing taste. It has a deep-rooted popularity in Japan.

▲ **Japanese Sweets (wagashi)** Sweets in Japan are intended to satisfy both the sight and the taste. There is also pleasure in the seasonal feeling they evoke.

▲ **Oden** An example of nabemono popular in Japan since the Edo period. Two main types are recognized: one made on a broth based on soy sauce, the other made on a broth based on *miso* (fermented bean paste). It is a style of cooking growing popular overseas.

●Kaiseki ryori (informal banquet cooking)

Japanese cooking reached maturity during the Edo period, supported by the development of restaurants and by the existence of other cooking traditions such as the European (*nanban ryori*, mainly Dutch, Spanish and Portuguese) and the Chinese.

With the existence of restaurants and the growth in the social influence of urban dwellers (*chonin*), relaxed and informal dinner parties became very popular, and the food served at them incorporated the forms and content of both *honzen ryori* and *chakaiseki*, though taste was emphasized over the formalities. This newly developed, independent form of cooking was called *kaiseki* (banquet) *ryori*.

By the end of the Edo period, when restaurants had become firmly established in the culture, both the food and the number of courses served became more sumptuous. The small tables on which the food was served (*zen*) changed also, becoming legless trays called *kaisekizen*.

●Gyoji ryori (food associated with annual events)

Since ancient times, special food has traditionally been prepared for festivals and celebrations. The assortment of food called *osechi ryori*, cooked ahead and served in special lacquered boxes, and the special soup called *ozoni* appear at the New Year, and the boxed food (*orizume*) is served at celebrations and ceremonies. Even today, when the national diet is so much richer and more varied than that of people of the past, the Japanese retain a special affection for the food that in the past contrasted strongly in its extravagance with the simple food of every day.

▲*Osechi ryori* Sumptuous New Year's food. Traditionally the food has been arranged as shown in five-layered lacquer boxes called *jubako*. The norm nowadays however is for only two or three layers. There are many local traditions in *osechi ryori*; the type shown here is from Tokyo.

▼(right) **Boxed Food** The items, of an auspicious uneven number, are packed in a box, which is wrapped with thick ceremonial paper, and tied with strands of decorative string dyed red and white.

▲*Ozoni* A soup integral to the cooking that celebrates the New Year. It is essentially a soup containing glutinous rice cakes called *mochi*, garnished with a variety of other ingredients. Different regions have different ways of shaping the *mochi*, of selecting the other ingredients and of seasoning. The photograph shows four different types rich in local color.

▲**Boxed Food** The sea bream cooked whole and the red rice (*sekihan*) are the core of celebratory food. Here, they are packed to be taken home with the guest. Red rice is made by steaming small red *azuki* beans with glutinous rice.

●Modern Japanese Cooking

We cannot speak of modern Japanese cooking without considering the ubiquitous role of the restaurant in Japanese culture. It is not an exaggeration to say that traditional forms and dishes are now the preserve of high-class restaurants and inns, or are served only on ceremonial occasions, such as wedding banquets.

Nevertheless, a new type of Japanese cooking style has emerged which in its modern outlook sensitively reflects the spirit of the times. While taking into account traditional methods of preparation, it has adopted new ingredients, as well as an eclectic style which brings out the best in Western and Chinese cooking.

Of course there are many specialty restaurants serving well-loved traditional dishes, such as sushi, tempura, unagi (eel), soba and udon (two types of noodles). At the same time restaurants in general today are the setting for the diversification and internationalization of Japanese cooking. Large numbers of Western and Chinese restaurants, as well as fast-food outlets, compete with each other and with the traditional Japanese places, acting as a spur to one another. Japan must be the leading country in the world for multi-cultural cooking.

The table of the average family is, at least in the metropolitan areas, similarly diversified and multifaceted, and traditional home cooking is gradually being eroded.

▲**Packed lunch** *(bento)* One type is used for taking on excursions, etc. and another for formal dining. The type pictured is the *Shokado bento*, most often eaten at tea ceremonies as *kaiseki*. Seasonal food is delicately wrought and arranged.

●Eating Etiquette

When eating traditional food, such as formal *chakaiseki* or *honzen*, the etiquette and the rules are strict and detailed. From how to set down the lid of your soup bowl and how to place your chopsticks on the table to the order of consumption of the dishes and the way to bring the meal to a finish, everything has a particular formality.

However, when enjoying ordinary food, this formality tends to be little regarded, and the enjoyment of the cooking itself is foremost. Rather than learning formal etiquette, what is more important is the spirit in which the food is served, as expressed in the cooking, and the effort given to sincere appreciation of the beauty and the taste of the food. Here are some basic pointers which presuppose such a frame of mind.

Firstly, eat what is supposed to be hot while it is still hot, and do not let what is supposed to be cold get warm. That is both politeness to the cook and appreciation of the food at its best.

Japanese food is to be consumed by the eyes as well as the tongue. Before and while eating, take your time to appreciate the beauty, the freshness and the smell of the food.

Slurping your soup is not necessarily rude, but avoid talking with your mouth full.

Cultural differences in eating and cooking may mean that some food does not agree with you. Nevertheless, as far as possible, try not to leave any food.

Eating is a pleasure, and conversation is a part of that pleasure. It is good to be stimulated by conversation, but be careful not to let it dominate your meal, and not to speak in such a loud voice that it disturbs people at other tables.

These are merely some ways to make the meal more pleasant; there is no need to think of them in over-formal terms.

●The Use of Chopsticks and Japanese Cooking

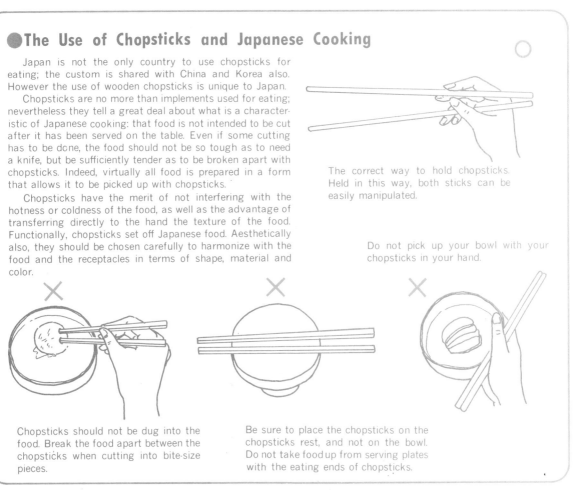

Japan is not the only country to use chopsticks for eating; the custom is shared with China and Korea also. However the use of wooden chopsticks is unique to Japan.

Chopsticks are no more than implements used for eating; nevertheless they tell a great deal about what is a characteristic of Japanese cooking: that food is not intended to be cut after it has been served on the table. Even if some cutting has to be done, the food should not be so tough as to need a knife, but be sufficiently tender as to be broken apart with chopsticks. Indeed, virtually all food is prepared in a form that allows it to be picked up with chopsticks.

Chopsticks have the merit of not interfering with the hotness or coldness of the food, as well as the advantage of transferring directly to the hand the texture of the food. Functionally, chopsticks set off Japanese food. Aesthetically also, they should be chosen carefully to harmonize with the food and the receptacles in terms of shape, material and color.

The correct way to hold chopsticks. Held in this way, both sticks can be easily manipulated.

Do not pick up your bowl with your chopsticks in your hand.

Chopsticks should not be dug into the food. Break the food apart between the chopsticks when cutting into bite-size pieces.

Be sure to place the chopsticks on the chopsticks rest, and not on the bowl. Do not take food up from serving plates with the eating ends of chopsticks.

FORETHOUGHT AND MINIATURIZATION

Forethought

Forethought is a distinctive feature of Japanese behavior. What the word expresses is a variation on the Golden Rule: to do unto others—usually for their benefit —before being asked to do so. Typical examples will clarify how it works.

◇ **A Lockless Culture** Western-style doors have locks on them, as do Japanese doors that open to the outside. But *fusuma* and *shoji*—the room dividers in a Japanese house—are not so equipped. Neither is it a conventional practice in Japan to ask permission each time one wishes to enter a room. Faced with a closed *fusuma*, the only recourse for the would-be entrant is to employ forethought to interpret whether the closed *fusuma* means "Keep Out", "Knock First", or "Ask". Without such forethought, *fusuma* would be unable to

fulfill its function as a boundary marker.

◇ **Non-Verbal Communication** Rather than use words or argument to gain another's understanding, the Japanese prefer to convey their intentions or feelings through subtle signals using a minimum of verbal communication. Words, say the Japanese, are merely signals that indicate directions and function no more than signs do. This is particularly evident in the family, where, among people who understand one another, outward demonstrations of affection such as hugging, kissing or verbal reassurances of love are neither the norm nor missed.

Even at the work place, associates of long standing most often convey their feelings through such non-verbal methods as head movements or altering facial expressions, and refrain from any long stream of personal questions. For people in close rela-

● **Determining attitude based on circumstances**

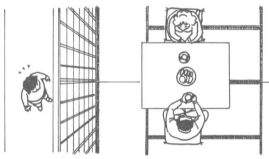

▲ "My brother has his girlfriend with him in his room; we'd better not call out to him."

● **What can be understood without words should not be voiced.**

▲ "Dad loves mom, but he has never once said 'I love you.' to her."

● **Something small which represents the whole world**

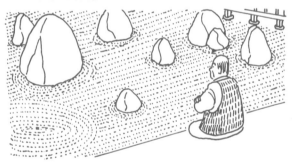

▲ This garden is a miniature of the universe. Small as it is, it contains mountains and seas.

● **Small is efficient.**

▲ Ever since the small but efficient transistor radio was put on the market in August 1955, a great variety of miniaturized products have made their appearance.

tionships, this is deemed sufficient to convey the message.

Small is Better

There are those who say that Japan is a country of the miniature culture; that is, a culture that makes small things—or makes things small. The Japanese, to be sure, have often enough failed when attempting expansion; but they have attained great success when it comes to reduction. Even traditional culture offers examples of this, as in *bonsai*. It is, so to speak, a knack the Japanese have for utilizing limited space as if it were limitless.

◇**Mechanical Miniatures**   The first item successfully miniaturized in the postwar industrial period was the portable radio. Next came the radio-cassette, then the miniaturized cassette tape-recorder, followed by a long list of small or compact items that includes the "Walkman", pocket calculators, TVs, cameras, cars and personal computers.

Haiku and Tanka

Haiku and *Tanka* are two traditional forms of poetry. *Haiku* is made up of 17 syllables, *Tanka* 31. These ever-popular art forms are enjoyed by young and old, male and female in all walks of life. To create an image in only 17 or 31 syllables requires that the words used be carefully chosen for their succinctness, be pared down to bare essentials, and be symbolically expressive of the feeling to be evoked:

> Matsushima ya
> Ah, Matsushima ya
> Matsushima ya

By the simple repetition of the name "Matsushima", treating it almost like an interjection, the poem attempts to capture the scenic beauty of the Matsushima area, which is well-nigh impossible to put into words.

●The *haiku*—a poem in seventeen syllables

荒 海 や（5 syllables）
Ah, the rough sea!

佐 渡 に 横 た う（7 syllables）
And, stretching over Sado Island,

天 の 河（5 syllables）
the, Galaxy.

▲Matsuo Basho (1644-1694), the most famous of the *haiku* poets, brought the world's vastness into a short poem of seventeen syllables.

●BONSAI

Bonsai is nature in a small package. Interest in bonsai among gardening enthusiasts abroad is such that the word now has an international currency.

Bonsai is the attempt to portray the macro cosmos on a micro scale. A solitary pine or other tree, or a grouping of various plants is placed in a pot, tray or some such container along with rocks, soil or sand. A tiny stand of trees can thus be likened to the grandeur of nature's own forests—an exquisite miniature intended to expand in the mind's eye. It is the Japanese mind trying to find the mystery of the universe within the limited space of a tiny garden.

GESTURES AND ACTIONS

Pulling And Pushing

Gestures intended to convey the same meanings often differ greatly from country to country, as is evident even in the motions of pushing and pulling. It is said the basic movement in the West, whether in the use of tools or in gestures, is one of pushing. In Japan, the basic movement is one of pulling. Typical examples are the ways in which tools such as saws and planes are used. In Japan they are pulled to cut; in the West they are pushed.

Actions Easily Misunderstood

A cautionary word should be said in connection with some of the actions peculiar to Japan. In conversation, it is common for the listener to nod and utter approving sounds. These do not, however, necessarily mean consent or agreement. In fact, in most cases they signal only that the listener is receiving input; that the physical act of hearing is taking place.

Another potential source of misunderstanding is smiling. A Japanese, like most other people, will usually have a smile on his or her face when happy or amused. The problem is that the smile is sometimes there even when the person is sad or embarrassed. This may be due to mild or intense embarrassment, or to the fact that the person does not wish to reveal the extent of emotions raging within. According to Japanese thinking, disclosing such emotions would be to foist off one's problems onto another, to burden the listener and thereby show a lack of consideration.

Nodding and smiling in conversation are no more than long-established paralingual habits and should not be construed as malevolent or anything other than normal actions for a Japanese.

●The Cutting Motion with Japanese Implements

▲Japanese saws and planes are used with the blade edge facing toward the body and consequently the cutting motion toward the user, in contrast to the Western style of usage. Likewise, the Japanese sword does not cut in a thrusting motion like the European sword, but in a swing-draw motion.

●Counting on the Fingers

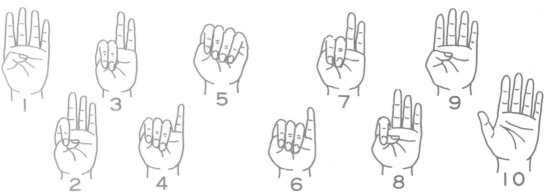

▲For the numbers 1 to 5, the fingers are bent in the order . thumb to little finger, and for the numbers 6 to 10, the fingers are raised in the order little finger to thumb.

●Indicating Numbers to Others

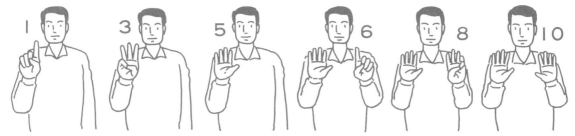

▲With the elbow bent, the hand raised, and the fingers bent as shown in the diagram. One hand is used for the numbers 1 to 5, and two hands when counting from 6 to 10.

●Indicating Oneself

▲When inquiring whether something is theirs, or indicating themselves, the Japanese point to their nose with their finger.

●Beckoning Someone

▲The palm of the hand faces downwards, the fingers are extended slightly, and the hand is waved several times in a beckoning motion towards the body of the beckoner. This is not a gesture that is performed toward a superior.

●Banzai

▲Equivalent to the English "three cheers," the word *banzai* is shouted three times in unison to the accompaniment of raised arms when someone has won a contest, when there is something to be celebrated, or when a party comes to a close.

●Maru and Batsu

▲Maru, the sign of a circle, indicates that something is correct. Its positive image contrasts with the negative of the batsu sign, a cross, which indicates that a mistake has been made.

●Shaking Hands and Bowing

▲The Japanese bow contrasts with the European and American custom of handshaking in that, instead of being based on the thrusting motion of the hand toward the greetee, the head is bowed and the body bent forward and withdrawn in modesty.

●WINKING

Like most nonverbal signals, winking has a significance that varies from society to society. In Japan's case, winking is not even a custom, so that the chances of observing one in action are just about nil. However, as observers of Western culture, many Japanese feel they understand the meaning of the wink. As the following story suggests, this assumption is open to question. A young Japanese girl on vacation in California was winked at by a handsome young man. Taking it to be a sign that he was personally interested in her, she had mixed feelings to discover that the wink he'd given her was simply a kind of conditioned reflex he would give to any attractive young girl, meaning no more than a visual way of saying a friendly hello.

GUESTS AND GIFTS

Entertaining Guests

The desire to do one's best when entertaining guests is universal. The considerable differences that exist across borders are only in regard to ways and methods. In the West, entertaining guests in the warmth of the home and serving them a home-cooked meal is usually preferred. Just the opposite is true in Japan where tradition prescribes that a meal prepared by a superb chef at a spacious and impressive restaurant is by far the superior way to treat a guest. However, nowadays it is becoming more common to invite people to one's home as in the Western fashion.

Japanese-Style Hospitality

In Japan, seeing to a guest's needs is an important part of serving as host. A host will try to anticipate what a guest might want or need. Coffee or tea, for example, will sometimes promptly be served a visitor automatically, and it would not be thought unusual if drinks or even a meal were brought out.

O-shibori, the small dampened cloth offered to guests at private homes, inns, restaurants and practically everywhere else, falls within this category of hospitality. Chilled in summer and warmed in winter, *o-shibori* provides a refreshing prelude to a meal, drinks, or conversation.

Gift-Giving

On even the simplest occasion a gift (o-miyage) is customarily taken along and presented as an expression of the giver's respect and goodwill.

Seasonal gifts are an important aspect of Japanese culture. O-chugen (mid-year gifts) is usually given to one's superiors from early June to mid July. O-seibo (year-end gifts) is presented as an expression of appreciation for favors received in the past year. Those in a socially superior position, such as a family doctor, or a teacher of flower arrangement are typical recipients. Today these gifts are delivered by stores or sent through the mail. Gift sets of seasonal foods and drinks, soap sets, and flowers are only some of such gifts. O-toshidama (New-

Year's gift) which had religious meaning in the past connected with Shinto or Buddhism is now always given to children in cash by parents and close relatives or by neighbors as a New Year's gift. Gift-giving is part of a larger system of social exchange.

●Some situations to be careful about

▲Do not take gifts that have roots attached, such as potted plants, when visiting a sick person. The Japanese dislike to receive anything that reminds them of "taking root," since it implies that the illness will be prolonged.

▲Do not open a present immediately upon receiving it. The Japanese have traditionally considered such behavior to be bad manners.

▲Whereas in Europe and America the custom is that neighbors welcome a newly arrived person with a gift, in Japan, the person who has moved in is expected to take a present to his or her new neighbors.

Significant stages in human life such as birth, coming of age, and marriage, as well as funerals and partings require gifts. Gifts are often given out of a sense of obligation and in turn require a return gift (O-kaeshi).

Saying Thank You

It may be considered rude for a receiver of another's hospitality (be it a meal, drinks or gifts) to thank his or her benefactor only once. "Arigato gozaimasu" (the polite form of "Thank you") is first said upon receiving them. Gratitude is expressed again when the recipient next meets the giver. This custom of saying "Thank you" several times conveys a perpetual rather than a transitory relationship between them.

●Sitting on *tatami* floors

• Seiza

• Informal Sitting Styles

▲*Seiza* is the formal way of sitting on *tatami*. Since the legs are tucked under one's body, they tend to fall asleep.

▲Men may sit cross-legged in informal situations, but women must sit with the legs tucked back on one side of the body or the other.

●Bowing in the Japanese fashion

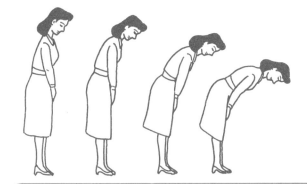

The basic form of greeting in Japan is the bow. When standing, bring the legs together, bend the body forward from the waist, and lower the head. The angle at which the head is lowered indicates the degree of politeness of the bow. When sitting on *tatami* matting, bow from the *seiza* position bending the whole body forward, placing both hands on the floor in front and lowering the head.

●Direct Ordering of Local Products

Gift-giving as an expression of thanks at prescribed seasons, known as *o-chugen* in mid-year and *o-seibo* at the year end, is a thriving custom in Japan. Such gifts may be given personally to the recipient, although in the majority of cases they are delivered by the department store with whom the order was placed. Since, however, there is little variation among the goods offered by the various department stores, the choice has tended to become stereotyped. In addition, many restrictions apply when sending fresh foodstuffs.

What has become popular in recent years is having local goods sent directly from the place of production by placing a telephone call, thus ensuring the freshness of the product. Since the early sixties such direct ordering has gained a following as a way of lowering costs by avoiding the usual distribution network of wholesaler and retailer, and a means by which health foods (e. g., those on which agricultural chemicals have not been used) may be obtained. It has only been more recently, however, that direct ordering of fresh foodstuffs or distinctive local products has been applied to the buying of seasonal gifts. The popularity of such direct ordering is gradually increasing, suiting as it does the Japanese national characteristic of love of fresh natural foods which suggest a particular season.

▲A variety of products bought by direct order

SEASONAL VARIATIONS AND HARMONY WITH NATURE

Seasonal Changes

Japan's seasons are clear-cut. Since the archipelago runs north and south some 3000 kilometers it encompasses both a semi-tropical and semi-frigid zone, providing the nation with weather of almost every sort: rainy, dry, snow, typhoons and most things in between.

Such a varied climate has fostered among the people a keen awareness of nature, as can be seen in various arts and customs. Nature, for example, is always an important theme in classical literature, with seasonal elements incorporated as essential background. And in the 17-syllable type of poetry known as *haiku*, words that indicate the seasons are indispensable components.

Endowed with a relatively mild marine climate and surrounded by sea, Japan, an island country, was shielded from a magnitude of calamities, natural or man-made. This fact has greatly influenced Japanese life and even formed the inclination referred to as "insular narrowness".

Nature in its Cultural Perception

The tea ceremony, flower arrangement, garden construction and many other arts exemplify the Japanese outlook toward nature. The essence of such arts is a reduced reproduction of nature as it is. Even in the martial arts the Japanese perception of nature can be seen. In judo, for example, the

●Traditional kimono patterns reflecting the seasons

Japanese kimonos are known the world over for the beauty of their patterns, which are abstractions of natural phenomena through the four seasons. Such patterns perfectly reflect the cast of the Japanese mind which delights in nature and feels close to it.

▼A spring kimono

▼A summer kimono

▼An autumn kimono

▼A winter kimono

opponent is brought down not by matching strength with strength, but by yielding to his strength and utilizing it so that the opponent falls from his own force.

Nature and the Commonplace

The attitude of harmonizing with nature is clearly evident in the daily things of life. A traditional Japanese house, for example, is made of wood, floored with *tatami*, and divided into rooms by *fusuma* and *shoji* partitions made of wood and paper. This is not inconvenient though it might at first seem so. Actually, it is the ideal construction given Japan's humid summer climate, as it allows for air circulation throughout the house and thus aids in controlling mold and mildew.

In regard to food there is much that, like *sashimi*, is eaten raw, and when food is cooked, great efforts are taken to preserve its natural appearance and flavor.

As Japanese life becomes more and more Westernized and urbanized there is a corresponding lessening of the spirit of harmonizing with nature. Houses these days are of concrete more often than not—albeit with Japanese adaptations—and processed and artificially grown foods rob the seasons of their unique offerings. Even so, given their preference, most Japanese would still opt for nature's way.

●Seasonal variation between north and south

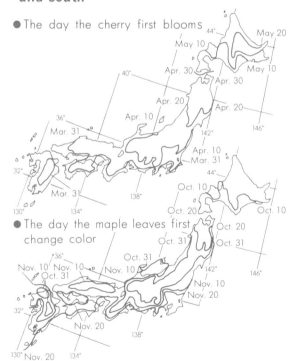

●The day the cherry first blooms

●The day the maple leaves first change color

Though Japan is a small country, it stretches some 3,000 kilometers north to south, over twenty-five degrees of latitude. As a result, there is a great difference in temperatures between north and south, and a forty-day variation between the times the cherry first blooms and between the times the maple leaves change color. Nevertheless, though the season may vary at any one time from place to place, cherry blossoms and maple leaves are to be found in every part of Japan, and Japanese people, wherever they may live in the archipelago, have a common feeling for nature, that the cherry is the symbol of spring and the maple the symbol of autumn.

●BATHING

The Japanese are a bath-loving people. There is, however, a difference in the way they take baths. All soaping, scrubbing and rinsing of the body is done outside the tub and usually while perched atop a tiny stool. Water disappears via a drain in the floor, which is usually of tile. Only after the body is thoroughly clean will a Japanese submerge neck-deep in the hot water of a deep tub to soak and relax. Though a shower might suffice in the West for the practical purpose of cleansing the body, a bath—a Japanese-style bath—is something no Japanese would willingly do without.

It is also the norm in Japan to bathe in the evening, usually before retiring. Again this is quite in contrast to the common Western practice of showering in the morning before leaving for the day's activities. Traditionally, the Japanese have believed that a morning bath is not suitable for the diligent. This idea has even found expression in an old folksong that bemoans the fate of one who loses everything because of being too fond of sleeping, drinking and bathing in the morning.

And yet when on vacation at a hot springs resort some Japanese do enjoy a morning bath—irresistibly nice! Due to numerous volcanoes throughout the nation spas have long abounded. Some even have facilities for open-air bathing. This allows the bather to relax both body and soul in natural surroundings while enjoying the scenic beauty. Such a style of bathing also underscores the Japanese predilection for harmonizing with nature. Meanwhile, there has been a decrease in the number of *sento*—the public bathing facilities that used to dot each neighborhood. Nevertheless they are still used as a kind of meeting-place for gossiping. Increasing numbers of foreign residents in Japan use these public baths.

▲Open-air bathing

LIFE OF A SALARIED EMPLOYEE

Many people abroad are under the impression that the average Japanese willingly slaves at the workplace. Are the Japanese truly such a hardworking people? History indicates that their ancestors were, since hard work was the only alternative for farmers who wanted the biggest harvests possible from their meager plots of land. Such historical factors conform well with today's emphasis on prosperity and success.

Due to the lifetime employment system, the corporate worker has a strong identification with the company. This in turn contributes to stability in management, for the company and employee both feel as if they are in the same boat. It is against this kind of background that Japan achieved its phenomenal economic growth in the 1960s.

Workaholics in Rabbit Hutches?

In view of their hard work it would seem that the Japanese are now enjoying "the good life". Young working singles can, it is true, indulge themselves in clothes and travel; but once married, they too come smack up against economic realities. Japan's status as a country with a huge trade surplus cannot erase the smallness of the nation's land or the scarcity of its natural resources. Japan's economy rests on a surprisingly fragile foundation. Its inadequacies compel the Japanese to be "workaholics". The epithet of affluence is belied by poor social welfare and unsatisfactory infrastructure, with personal assets comparatively lower than in Western countries. Under such circumstances the word "affluent" seems a misnomer. Housing—or more precisely its inadequacy—is a glaring example. Even to obtain what has jokingly been referred to as a "rabbit hutch" takes a lifetime of hard work for urban Japanese. With the price of land in metropolitan areas sky-rocketing, the dream of owning a home continues to be nothing more than just a dream.

A Day in the Life of a Salaried Man

Many workers in big cities spend over an hour commuting to their jobs each day on

●OCCUPATIONS AND CLOTHING

At one time in Japan, clothing specific to an occupation came about naturally by the wearers themselves. This has now all but disappeared and workers wear clothes more in keeping with the times and in tune with the rest of the world. In contrast, nurserymen, carpenters and a few other workers (see below) continue to wear traditional work clothes.

▶salaried worker

▲doctor

▼greengrocer

▲policeman

▼hairdresser

▼sushi shop employee

▲fish dealer

▲nurseryman

▲carpenter

▲farmer

▲fisherman

jam-packed trains. Once at the office they hear a morning pep talk or perhaps loudly chant the company's motto as a prelude to the day's work.

Employees often work overtime and without taking their alloted annual vacations. After work, they often stop off for a drink with colleagues to relax, exchange small talk and information, and get rid of the day's stress, all of which is considered helpful in business.

Nighttime can also mean entertaining company clients. This often involves bar-hopping and singing at *karaoke* (sing-along) bars.

Company Parties

Every year in April companies hire a new crop of employees, and each department or section holds drinking parties to welcome them. Such parties deepen the sense of belonging and help bond the new-comers to the group.

All of the year's frustrations, failures and disappointments are forgotten and only its pleasant memories are reminisced and toasted to at parties called *bonenkai* (year-end party). Such parties are usually held in mid-December. Their festive atmosphere

▲ Rush hour in Shinjuku station, Tokyo.

fosters a mutual desire to work together in the coming year.

The Pursuit of Leisure

During the industrial boom until some years ago, intensive production made it necessary for workers to dedicate much of their time to their jobs and the Japanese generally felt work was what made life worth-while. They spent their limited free time relaxing in front of the TV or playing a Japanese form of pinball called *pachinko*.

Nowadays, however, especially among the young, a strong shift towards active enjoyment of one's leisure hours in a more positive manner has occurred. Tennis and skiing are popular among the young set, while those in middle age and above find enjoyment and pleasure in such pursuits as golf, jogging, and weekend carpentry.

● **Weekly working hours in industry** (1984)

	(hours) 0	10	20	30	40
W. Germany				31,3	
France				31,7	
USA					37,0
England					37,4
Japan					41,7

● **Hourly wage in industry** (1984)

	(yen) 0	500	1,000	1,500	2,000	2,500
W. Germany					2,180	
USA			1,403			
Japan			1,293			
England			1,167			
France		812				

● **Number of days off**

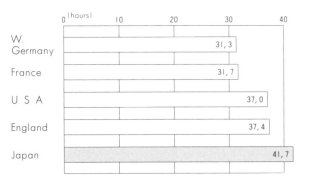

● **Distribution of commutation time** (weekdays)

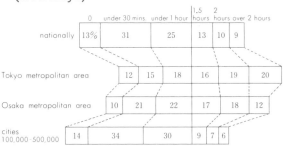

EDUCATION IN JAPAN

High Educational Level

Japan's high level of education has enabled it to become a prominent economic power despite its small size and lack of natural resources. Moreover, Japan can boast of being one of the most highly educated countries in the world, for at present school enrollment and literacy rates are 100%.

Japan's modern system of education had its beginnings in 1872 following the Meiji Restoration. But Japan's tradition of popular education goes back even further. In the latter half of the 18th century when the Tokugawa shoguns ruled the country, there was already a fairly developed system of private schools for the children of the warrior class and "temple schools" for the commoners. Around the middle of the 19th century, approximately 45% of male children and 15% of female children could read and write. These figures put Japan in proximity to the advanced countries of that era.

Nine Years of Mandatory Education

Primary learning was limited to four years when the compulsory education system was first established. It was later extended to six years and then to nine years after the Pacific War in 1947. Japan's present educational system requires six years of elementary school and three years of junior high school for a total of 9 years of compulsory learning. Enrollment is 100%. Although high school is not a part of mandatory education, Japan's competitive society makes it as if it were so. About 94% of junior high graduates go on to high school.

Above high school is the university, which offers four years of study. There are more than 460 universities; 95 are state institutions and 34 are public. Junior colleges, with two-year terms, number about 540. Some 37% of high school graduates go on to higher education. The four-year universities offer Graduate School Programs and have an enrollment of around 55,000 students.

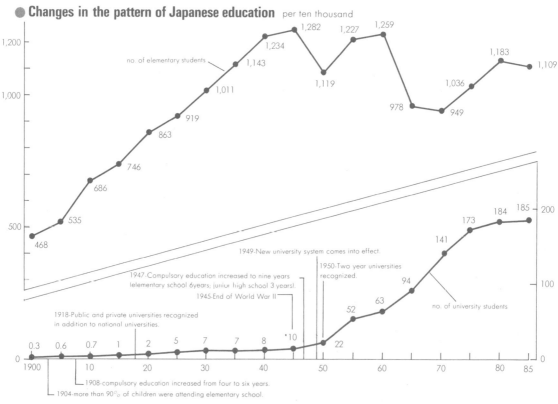

● **Changes in the pattern of Japanese education** per ten thousand

no. of elementary students

1,282 1,227 1,259 1,234 1,143 1,119 1,011 978 1,036 949 1,183 1,109

919 863 746 686 535 468

1949-New university system comes into effect.

1947-Compulsory education increased to nine years (elementary school 6years; junior high school 3 years).

1950-Two year universities recognized.

1945-End of World War II

1918-Public and private universities recognized in addition to national universities.

no. of university students

185 184 173 141 94 63 52 22

0.3 0.6 0.7 1 2 5 7 7 8 '10

1900 10 20 30 40 50 60 70 80 85

1908-compulsory education increased from four to six years.

1904-more than 90% of children were attending elementary school.

All schools begin in April, although a September entry is also being pursued in view of the need to accommodate numerous students from abroad and returning Japanese students.

"Examination Hell" and the "Juku" Boom

Japanese children must be among the busiest in the world, for many, if not most, attend "juku"(private tutoring schools) in addition to their regular studies. The reason for all this schooling is due to the difficult university entrance examinations.

Japan has long been a society that takes a person's academic background seriously. A person's alma mater (university) can be a determining factor in employment by a big-name firm, appointment to a high government position, or even assure promotion. Therefore entrance examinations to top-rated universities are so difficult that they are referred to as sheer "hell". Many parents send their children to "juku" which offer lessons in the academic subjects that are important in school entrance examinations, primarily English, mathematics, and Japanese. The rigorous "juku" require hard-er work and longer hours than ordinary schools. Japanese children are under great pressure in the present educational system. As a matter of fact some parents even believe that a good kindergarten is necessary to assure admission to a good elementary school and so on up the line.

Except for the positions of high-ranking government officials, the significance of one's academic background is gradually diminishing as more and more weight is being given to a worker's ability. The Japanese system of seniority is not actually employed to the extent believed abroad. Even so, many parents still think it best to enroll their children in good schools.

Youth in Search of Vocational Training

Increasing numbers of young people are forsaking a university education to study at professional or other specialty schools ranging from computer technology to cooking. Others attend university classes during the day and study at technical schools at night, a phenomenon referred to as "Double School".

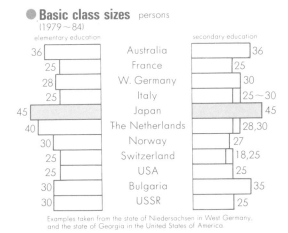

Basic class sizes persons
(1979~84)

Examples taken from the state of Niedersachsen in West Germany, and the state of Georgia in the United States of America.

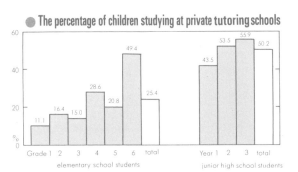

The percentage of children studying at private tutoring schools

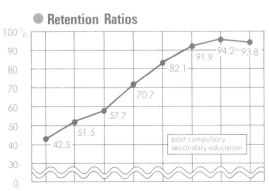

Retention Ratios

The percentage of junior high school graduates who continue on to study in senior high school.

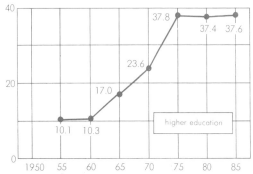

The percentage of senior high school graduates who continue on to study in four or two-year universities.

THE JAPANESE GOVERNMENT

Three Divisions of Power

Over the years a number of words or phrases about Japan have gained currency abroad, such as "harakiri" of the samurai, "kamikaze" of the Second World War or the "economic animal" of the '60s and '70s. Taken in the aggregate these terms would seem to suggest that Japan is a nation unsettled or exotic—whereas in truth it is the most stable democracy in Asia.

The organization of the Japanese government is patterned after the English parliamentary system. Political power is shared by three branches of government: the legislative power of the Diet, the administrative power of the cabinet, and the judicial power of the judiciary.

The Diet

The Diet is the most prominent of the three powers of government. It is made up of the House of Representatives (512 members serving four years) and the House of Councillors (252 members serving six years). Both houses are entirely elective. Although the powers of the two houses are similar, higher authority resides in the House of Representatives which can, for example, repass a bill rejected by the Councillors and announce it as the decision of the entire Diet. The House of Representatives can also initiate a non-confidence motion in the cabinet. Should it be passed, the cabinet must then resign en bloc or the House of Representatives be dissolved. In the latter case, the incumbency of the members terminates at that point.

The Cabinet

The Prime Minister heads the cabinet. He or she is elected by the members of the Diet. Since members ordinarily vote for the head of the party they are affiliated with, the head of the party holding the largest number of seats becomes Prime Minister. The Prime Minister represents Japan at important international conferences as the Emperor is only the symbolic head of state. Unlike the President of the United States, the Prime Minister is not elected directly by the people but indirectly through the strength of a political party.

Political Parties

The major political parties in Japan are the Liberal Democratic Party (LDP), the Social Democratic Party of Japan (SDPJ), the Komei Party, the Democratic Socialist Party, the Japan Communist Party (JCP), the Japan Renewal Party (JRP), the Japan New Party

▲The Diet Building

●Distribution of seats by party, House of Representatives (as at election)

date of election	The Liberal Democratic party	Japan Socialist party	Democratic Socialist party	Komei party	Japan Communist party	Other	full number
1958. 5	287	166			1	13	467
1960.11	296	145	17		3	6	467
1963.11	283	144	23		5	12	467
1967. 1	277	140	30	25	5	9	486
1969.12	288	90	31	47	14	16	486
1972.12	271	118	19	29	38	16	491
1976.12	249 (New Liberal Club 17)	123	29	55	17	21	511
1979.10	248 (4)	107 (United Social Democratic party 2)	35	57	39	19	511
1980. 6	284 (12)	107	32	33	29	3	511
1983.12	250 (8)	112	38	58	26	16 (3)	511
1986. 7	300 (6)	85	26	56	26	9 (4)	512

The New Liberal Club disbanded in August 1986; most of its members joined the Liberal Democratic party.

(JNP), and the Sakigake (Harbinger) Party. The LDP was formed in 1955 by the merger of earlier conservative parties, and enjoyed a monopoly of power in postwar politics for 38 years. The Prime Minister always came from the LDP, and the party contributed to the growth and stability of the nation. LDP scandals came to light one after another, and a number of members quit the party to establish new parties. As a result, the anti-LDP forces were able to form a coalition government in 1993 and the LDP has become Japan's leading opposition party.

Party Factions

A peculiarity of Japanese politics is the existence of factions within the party. The LDP contains five large ones, each formed mainly according to personal affiliations rather than major differences in policies or viewpoints. Faction leaders distribute funds to followers at election time and help loyal members obtain important positions within the party and cabinet. The faction leaders must be ardent fund-raisers and often place the interests of their constituencies above those of the nation at large. That such a conventional and premodern political mechanism should be so successful in creating one of the world's leading modern states is a matter of great interest.

●POLICE BOXES AND "SHAME CULTURE"

Crime usually rises as industrialization and urbanization progress, but such is not the case in Japan. Its crime rate in 1982 was at 1.2% as compared to 6% in the U.S. and other Western countries. Japan's criminal arrests were at nearly 60%, three times higher than in the U.S.

One contributing factor is Japan's "shame culture". The Japanese try to live up to an ideal image of themselves and when they fail, they feel ashamed of themselves in their own eyes as well as others'. Shame is a reaction to the feeling that one has disgraced one's own self-image. More practically, crime reduction is largely due to the low unemployment rate and the police box system. Scattered throughout cities and towns, police boxes consisting of one to five policemen form a system in which officers are able to immediately respond to situations because they routinely patrol their areas.

Police also kindly assist people who have lost their way or their belongings, and sometimes look after lost children, etc.

▲Police box

●The Japanese Political System

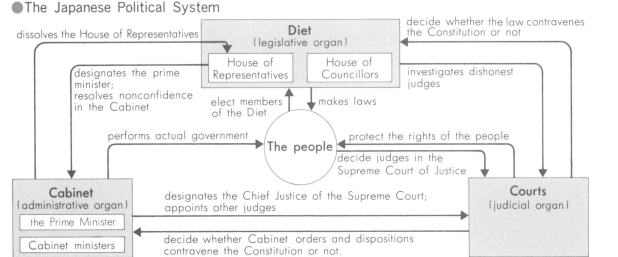

● Since the Cabinet is formed by the majority party, the people can, when dissatisfied with the Cabinet, express their will by not returning the majority party to power in elections.

● The House of Representatives has the power to designate the Prime Minister. Its authority exceeds that of the House of Councillors to vote for bills and the budget and to approve treaties.

MASS MEDIA

Newspapers Three characteristics of Japanese newspapers are the following: (1) Some are nationwide. (2)A clear-cut stance in regard to articles is avoided. (3)The publisher (not the reporter) assumes responsibility for published contents.

◇**Nationwide Newspapers** Japan's size makes news coverage easy. Since so much news is common to the country as a whole, nationwide papers play an important role. The three major national papers and their circulations (morning and evening editions combined) are: the *Yomiuri Shimbun* (13, ·740,000), the *Asahi Shimbun* (12,200,000), and the *Mainichi Shimbun* (6,400,000). Both the *Yomiuri* and the *Asahi* boast circulations extraordinarily high for privately-owned newspapers, surpassing the 10,000,000 circulation of the Soviet Union's *Pravda*. Local newspapers in Japan, on the other hand, cover local news in detail but have limited scope and influence.

◇**Factual Reportage Only** Newspaper reports, as opposed to those on TV, can express the views of a paper through the arrangement of editorials and columns. Generally speaking, however, Japanese newspapers avoid stating any clear-cut position on issues. This is because the pages of a newspaper are looked upon as a public forum and news as public property. Insistence on one's own views in such a situation is not something the Japanese public would be able to easily accept. This contrasts with the U.S., where newspapers are expected to clearly express where they stand on issues.

◇**Dubious Responsibility** Due to the public nature of newspapers, subjective reporting is avoided. Basically, each and every article is a neutral statement by the publisher. Criticism from the public is thus directed against the publisher, not the reporter. Though freed from the brunt of public censure, the reporter must, by the

● **Major newspapers worldwide and their circulation** (1985)

country	newspaper	circulation (in 1000s)	
Japan	Yomiuri Shimbun	morning paper	8 924
"	Asahi Shimbun	"	7 591
"	Mainichi Shimbun	"	4 180
USA	New York Daily News	"	1 353
"	The New York Times	"	963
England	Daily Mirror	"	3 169
"	Daily Express	"	1 883
"	Daily Mail	"	1 829
"	Times	"	458
France	France Soir	evening paper	433
W. Germany	Bild	morning paper	6 346
Italy	Corriere della Sera	"	583
USSR	Izvestia	evening paper	7 000
"	Pravda	morning paper	10 700
China	Renmin Ribao	"	5 700

Most newspapers in other countries tend to be either morning or evening papers. In Japan, however, the majority of newspapers put out both morning and evening editions. The circulations of evening editions of major newspapers are: Yomiuri Shimbun (4.82 million), Asahi Shimbun (4.61 million) and Mainichi Shimbun (2.21 million).

● **Number of publications issued**   100 millions

No. of new periodicals

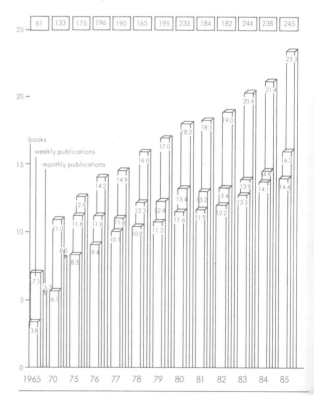

same token, work within the framework of editorial policy.

Weekly Magazines Weekly magazines rank with newspapers as print media. They can roughly be divided into socio-political magazines and entertainment magazines. The personal opinions expressed in the socio-political weeklies actually complement newspapers. Entertainment weeklies, on the other hand, sensationalize topics of personal interest and tend to be vulgar. Photo weeklies are a new kind of magazine. They purport to reveal the truth through articles composed of a single photo and a bit of sarcasm. Despite their spectacular popularity, their publishers are being called into question for their doubtful methods of gathering news and the flagrant way they cater to the public in their intense competition for sales.

Television Television broadcasting is conducted by the Nihon Hoso Kyokai (NHK) and commercial stations. Programs via NHK can be viewed nationwide.

Unlike commercial stations, NHK uses funds collected through users' fees based on a quasi-mandatory contract between all TV owners and NHK. An inevitable result of this operational framework is that the commercial stations cater to the masses.

Regulations governing program content are not excessively strict, so that sex and violence easily find their way over the airwaves.

In Tokyo, NHK has two channels: one for general programming, the other for programs of an educational nature. Commercial stations account for five channels: NTV, TBS, FUJI, TV ASAHI, and TV TOKYO.

Radio Radio broadcasting, like television, is conducted by NHK and commercial stations. Programs that teach conversational French, German, Chinese, Korean and other foreign languages are broadcast daily, with a particularly high audience rating for the Introductory English Conversation program. Late-night broadcasting by commercial stations finds a receptive audience among young people. Radio's portability also makes it a widely-used medium.

● **Number of books published (worldwide)** (1983) units

country	total	country	total
USSR	82 589	China	31 602
USA	76 976	Brazil	19 179
W. Germany	58 489	Canada	19 063
England	50 981	Italy	13 718
Japan	42 977	The Netherlands	13 324
France	37 576	Switzerland	11 405
Rep. of Korea	35 512	Yugoslavia	10 931
Spain	32 138	India	10 649

A unit is a single title. Periodicals are excluded.

● **Breakdown of television programs** (1986)

NHK (general television): news 38.0% | general culture 27.0% | entertainment 22.1% | education 12.9%

NHK (educational television): 20.1% | news 2.0% | general culture | education 77.9%

commercial television: news 16.6% | general culture 23.7% | entertainment 41.9% | education 12.1% | 5.7% other

● **Changes in the distribution of advertising among the media** yen

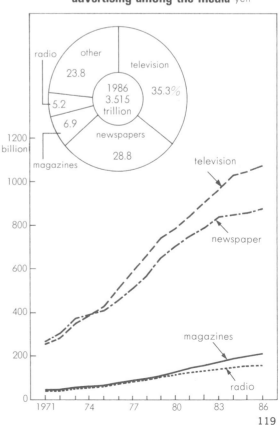

radio 23.8 / other / television 35.3% / 1986 3.515 trillion / magazines 5.2 / 6.9 / newspapers 28.8

television, newspaper, magazines, radio

1971 74 77 80 83 86

JAPANESE

Japanese is written in three styles of letters: *kanji*, *hira-gana*, and *kata-kana*.

Kanji

Kanji are characters borrowed from China, and each of them has its own meaning. Many *kanji* have meanings that derive from their shape. For example, 【日】 (sun) originated from a crude shape of the sun 【 ☼ 】. 【木】 (tree) came from 【 🌳 】. The character 【東】 (east) is a combination of the sun behind a tree 【 🌳 】, and 【田】 (rice paddy) is derived from four small fields 【 ⊞ 】. The character for man 【男】 came from the idea of a man supporting a field. The *kanji* for person 【人】 was taken from the pose of a standing man 【 🧍 】. In appearance it looks as if two bars are supporting each other. This character 【人】 symbolizes the idea that life is led in cooperation with others, that no one can live without the help of others, for if one bar is removed, the other falls.

Kanji are said to number about 50,000. Of these, 1,945 have been chosen as characters for everyday use. These are the ones that appear in newspapers, business letters, or official publications. However, there are other *kanji* that are used in personal and place names, so a knowledge of about 3,000 *kanji* is actually required.

Hira-gana and Kata-kana

Both *hira-gana* and *kata-kana* are phonetic syllabic scripts made from *kanji*. *Hira-gana* are actually simplified versions of selected *kanji*. *Kata-kana*, on the other hand, are segments extracted from whole *kanji*. Further information is provided in the chart on the facing page. Both *hira-gana* and *kata-kana* are original Japanese characters created in the 10th century. Each group has 46 basic letters, representing the basic sounds of the Japanese language.

Aspects of Japanese

Particles indicate the function of each word in a sentence. Although the subject of the sentence usually comes first and the predicate must come last, particles enable Japanese word order to be less rigid than that of English.

● The formation of *Kanji* (Chinese characters)

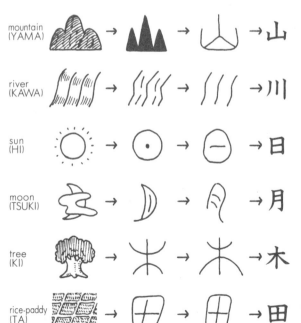

mountain (YAMA)

river (KAWA)

sun (HI)

moon (TSUKI)

tree (KI)

rice-paddy (TA)

Characters derived from pictorial representation

● A character formed by combining two simple characters

● 田 ＋ 力 ＝ 男 (OTOKO)

rice-paddy　　strength　　man

"Man," defined as one who works hard in the ricefields, is represented by a combination of the characters for "paddy" and "strength."

● 木 ＋ 木 ＝ 林 (HAYASHI)

tree　　　　tree　　　　woods

● 木 ＋ 木 ＋ 木 ＝ 森 (MORI)

tree　　　tree　　　tree　　　forest

A few trees make a wood, many a forest.

● 女 ＋ 家 ＝ 嫁 (YOME)

woman　　house　　bride

A bride is a woman who enters another family (house).

●The formation of kata-kana

	a	ka	sa	ta	na	ha	ma	ya	ra	wa	n
a	阿→阝→ア	加→カ→カ	散→サ→サ	多→タ→タ	奈→ナ→ナ	八→ハ→ハ	末→マ→マ	也→セ→ヤ	良→ラ→ラ	和→ワ→ワ	(ン)→ン→ン
i	伊→イ→イ	幾→キ→キ	之→シ→シ	千→チ→チ	二→ニ→ニ	比→ヒ→ヒ	三→ミ→ミ		利→リ→リ		
u	宇→ウ→ウ	久→ク→ク	須→ス→ス	川→ツ→ツ	奴→ヌ→ヌ	不→フ→フ	牟→ム→ム	由→ユ→ユ	流→ル→ル		
e	江→エ→エ	介→ケ→ケ	世→セ→セ	天→テ→テ	祢→ネ→ネ	部→ヘ→ヘ	女→メ→メ		礼→レ→レ		
o	於→オ→オ	己→コ→コ	曽→ソ→ソ	止→ト→ト	乃→ノ→ノ	保→ホ→ホ	毛→モ→モ	与→ヨ→ヨ	呂→ロ→ロ	呼→ヲ→ヲ	

Kata-kana were formed from one part of a Chinese character.

●The formation of hira-gana

	a	ka	sa	ta	na	ha	ma	ya	ra	wa	n
a	安→あ→あ	加→か→か	左→さ→さ	太→た→た	奈→な→な	波→は→は	末→ま→ま	也→や→や	良→ら→ら	和→わ→わ	无→ん→ん
i	以→い→い	幾→き→き	之→し→し	知→ち→ち	仁→に→に	比→ひ→ひ	美→み→み		利→り→り		
u	宇→う→う	久→く→く	寸→す→す	川→つ→つ	奴→ぬ→ぬ	不→ふ→ふ	武→む→む	由→ゆ→ゆ	留→る→る		
e	衣→え→え	計→け→け	世→せ→せ	天→て→て	祢→ね→ね	部→へ→へ	女→め→め		礼→れ→れ		
o	於→お→お	己→こ→こ	曽→そ→そ	止→と→と	乃→の→の	保→ほ→ほ	毛→も→も	与→よ→よ	呂→ろ→ろ	遠→を→を	

Hira-gana were formed by simplifying the forms of Chinese characters.

●SET EXPRESSIONS

Words of salutation such as *dozo yoroshiku* (I'm pleased to meet you.), or *o-sewa-ni-narimasu* (Please take care of me.), or *kochira koso* (I expect your kindness, too.) are but three of the many set phrases frequently spoken by the Japanese. No particular requests are made by the people involved; the speakers are simply acknowledging a relationship of mutual dependency.

Oftentimes important words are omitted in many Japanese set phrases. In *sayonara*, for example, which literally means "If so, then...", the idea of "I will see you again" is understood but not stated. The same is true for *kon-nichi-wa*, (literally, "this day"), used as a form of greeting. The full expression is "<u>This</u> <u>day</u> is a nice day."

And when a host serves food or drinks to company at home, he or she will say, much to the surprise of a foreign guest, "Nani mo arimasen ga, dozo meshiagatte kudasai"(This is nothing, but I hope you accept it.) What is understood but not spoken is, "This is nothing <u>THAT</u> <u>I</u> <u>CAN</u> <u>BRAG</u> <u>ABOUT</u>, but..." Set phrases like these express an attitude of modesty.

Nanimo arimasenga, dozo meshiagatte kudasai.

This is nothing, but I hope you accept it.

A Japanese lady

A foreign guest

A Japanese boy who speaks poor English.

Glossary of Culture and History

Asuka culture

The culture associated with Asuka, a region in the southern Yamato plain. It lasted from the middle of the 6th century, when Buddhism was transmitted to Japan, until the middle of the 7th century, the time of the Taika Reform. At its center was the Buddhism made popular by the regent Prince Shotoku (574-622), and it also exhibits Chinese, Indian and Hellenistic influences. The major artifacts extant from the time include the Horyuji, the Shakyamuni triad made by the sculptor Tori Busshi, the Kudara Kannon statue and the Tamamushi Portable Shrine.

Buddhism

The religion and a philosophical system of thought founded in the 6th century B. C. in India by Shakyamuni. Having realized enlightenment, Shakyamuni was called the Buddha ("the Enlightened One"), and his teachings on how to achieve a similar realization gradually spread throughout India, and south-east and east Asia. Buddhism teaches that to escape the delusion of this world it is necessary to possess both wisdom and compassion. It was transmitted from continental Asia to Japan in the 6th century and eventually extended its influence widely on politics and culture.

Bunjinga

Literati painting. A form of painting using ink and light colors, which was popular in the 18th and 19th centuries among scholars and writers. The style, poetic and unworldly, was much admired by the intellectuals of the time. Famous proponents of the form were Ike no Taiga (1723-1776), Yosa Buson (1716-1783) and Tanomura Chikuden (1777-1835).

Bushido

(lit. "the way of the warrior") A moral system taught among samurai, members of the warrior class, during the Edo period. It derived from the practical ethics held in common by samurai, such as the importance of loyalty, bravery, propriety, and frugality. It became theorized in the Edo period under the influence of Confucianism, especially the Neo-Confucianism of the Chu Hsi school, and established as the ethical ideal. Bushido, stripped of the most extreme of its militaristic, antimodern aspects, was once presented as a vehicle to define for Western people all that was most admirable in the Japanese tradition in politeness, generosity, honor, loyalty and self-control. Bushido's strong spiritualism, however, led Japan into becoming, in a

sense, an ultranationalistic state in the modern warring period. Some go as far as to say that Bushido represents all that was most despicable in Japanese wartime behavior. Most Japanese disowned Bushido as part of the ideological equipment of the militarists who had led Japan to defeat and humiliation in World War II and as incompatible with their postwar democratic society.

Byodoin

A temple at Uji, southeast of Kyoto, known particularly for its Amida Hall, popularly called the Phoenix Hall. It was originally the site of a country retreat on the banks of the Uji river, and was converted into a temple by the powerful statesman, Fujiwara no Yorimichi (992-1074), in 1052. The popular name of Phoenix Hall was given to the Amida Hall because of the Phoenix shape of its plan, and the ornaments in the shape of a Phoenix that decorate the roof. Built in 1053, the hall enshrines a statue of the Buddha Amitabha as the central image.

Castles

Military fortifications for protection against the attack of enemies. The number built in Japan increased rapidly after the 14th century, when local conflicts grew more and more widespread. Castles of that period were built on hill-tops, utilizing natural formations. As a result of developments in military techniques, in the 15th and 16th centuries large castles came to be built on the plains as well. They were surrounded by high stone walls and by moats, and became the center for the development of surrounding settlements, called castle towns.

Confucianism

A philosophical tradition attributed to the Chinese teacher Confucius who lived in the 6th century B. C. Confucius advocated that the state should be governed according to an ethical system that all people should uphold. His teachings flourished during the Han dynasty (202 B. C.-220 A. D.), when they were raised to the position of a state cult. A Neo-Confucian movement developed later, the Chu Hsi school during the Sung dynasty (960-1279), and the Wang Yang-ming school during the Ming dynasty (1368-1644). Confucianism exerted an enormous influence on the warrior class, and it was the ethical system that supported the feudal system of the Edo period.

Daimyo

Land-holding lords. The daimyo emerged as vassals of provincial governors in the

● Castles

Kumamoto Castle

Kochi Castle

Nagoya Castle

Kamakura period. During the civil war period of the 15th and 16th centuries, they assumed direct control of their territories. Though warfare, both offensive and defensive, was a way of life for the daimyo, they also encouraged local development by expanding agriculture and permitting the growth of settlements around their castles, the embryo castle town. During the Edo period, a daimyo was a member of the military class who had holdings worth more than 10,000 *goku* (one *koku* = 180 liters). There were three types: the *shimpan*, close relatives of the Tokugawa, the *fudai*, hereditary vassals, and the *tozama* (lit. "outside lords"), those who had previously been vassals of Nobunaga or Hideyoshi and who had sworn allegiance to the Tokugawa after 1600. In the early part of the Edo period many had their holdings reassigned. All *daimyo* were placed under the provisions of the Laws for Military Houses (*Buke Shohatto*) and were required to accede to the requirement of alternative attendance (*sankin kotai*); consequently their autonomy was circumscribed and they were subject to much shogunal intervention and control.

Edo Castle
The residence of fifteen generations of Tokugawa shoguns in what is now Tokyo. A small fortification had been built on the site by a local power holder, Ota Dokan (1432-1486) in the 15th century. In 1590 Tokugawa Ieyasu took possession of the castle at the order of his overlord, Toyotomi Hideyoshi, and began massive extensions. The Tokugawa surrendered it to imperial forces in 1868, and the following year it became the Imperial palace.

Emakimono
A scroll depicting a story in both pictures and words. It may be considered a type of Yamato-e (Yamato Painting), and was a popular art form in the 12th and 13th centuries. Famous examples include the *Genji Monogatari Emaki* (The picture scroll of the Tale of Genji) and the *Choju Giga* (The Scroll of the Frolicking Animals).

Esoteric Buddhism (Mikkyo)
A form of Buddhism that emphasizes the direct transmission of the teachings to attain enlightenment from master to disciple. These teachings attach great importance to demanding ascetic practice, prayers and incantations. Esoteric Buddhism rose in India in the 7th and 8th centuries and was brought to Japan early in the 9th century from T'ang China by the Japanese monks Kukai and Saicho. The former made esoteric teachings the center of his Shingon sect, and the latter incorporated them into his Tendai sect.

Fusuma-e
Pictures painted on *fusuma* (wooden sliding partitions), walls and *shoji*. The form was developed during the Momoyama period as internal decoration of castles and mansions. Members of the Kano school of painting in particular were responsible for flamboyant works using bright colors on a background of gold leaf.

Genroku culture
The culture that bloomed during the Genroku era (1688-1704). The newly rich and influential merchants of the Osaka, Kyoto regions were the driving force behind the vigorous and showy culture that combined the cultural traditions of Kyoto and the money of Osaka. The illustrated novels of Ihara Saikaku (1642-1693), the *joruri* scripts of Chikamatsu Monzaemon (1653-1724), and the *haikai* of Matsuo Basho (1644-1694) were all a product of this time. The culture eventually spread throughout the country.

Ginkaku
The Silver Pavilion. A two-storied building, part of the summer retreat erected in the Higashiyama district of Kyoto by the 8th Muromachi shogun, Ashikaga Yoshimasa (1436-1490), in 1489. Its name derives from the fact that original plans were for it to be covered with silver leaf. The lower storey is in the *shoen* style, and the upper is the Zen temple-hall style. With its surrounding garden, it is the epitome of Higashiyama culture. After Yoshimasa's death in 1490, the retreat was converted into a Buddhist temple, Jishoji.

Haikai
A poetic form derived from the classical thirty-one syllable verse form (*tanka*) and the prototype of the *haiku*. It grew out of the opening stanza (*hokku*) of linked verse (*renga*), and consists of three lines and seventeen syllables in the pattern 5-7-5. Despite its being very popular, it was considered slightly vulgar until refined by Matsunaga Teitoku (1571-1653), though with some loss of its original humor and spontaneity. Matsuo Basho brought the form to maturity in the late 17th century. (see also *haiku*)

Haiku
A poetic form also known as *haikai*. The term *haiku* was popularized by the poet Masaoka Shiki (1867-1902) and it is now used to designate the independent 5-7-5 syllable verse. It follows certain conventions, such as the use of a seasonal expression. Matsuo Basho combined the spontaneity of the *haikai* with artistic refinement and sensibility. He also introduced to it the aesthetic value of *sabi* (austere beauty). Other important poets were Yosa Buson

●Edo Castle

now Imperial palace

●Ginkaku

(1716-1783), Kobayashi Issa (1763-1827) and Masaoka Shiki. The form remains widely popular today.

Heiankyo

The original name of Kyoto, and the site of the capital of Japan, the center of government and the location of the imperial court for approximately 1100 years from its founding in 794, when the Emperor Kammu moved the capital there in an effort to reinvigorate the system of government based on the centralization of administration and taxation that was adopted after the Taika Reforms, until 1868 when the capital was shifted to Tokyo.

Patterned after the Chinese capital of Ch'ang-an, Heiankyo measured 4.5 kilometers from east to west and 5.3 kilometers from north to south, somewhat larger than the previous capital of Heijokyo (Nara). The emperor's residence and the government offices were to be located in the center of the city, the main avenues constructed on a grid system and the smaller streets also built to follow the same basic plan. However construction was brought to a halt in 805, and the city never achieved the form of the original plan.

Heijokyo

The capital built by the Empress Gemmei in what is now the western part of the city of Nara, patterned after the grid pattern of the Chinese capital of Ch'ang-an. For seventy-four years (710-784) it flourished as the center of government and culture. It measured about 4.2 kilomters from east to west, and about 4.7 kilometers from north to south. The residence of the emperor and the government offices were located in the northern part of the city and the main east-west and north-south avenues intersected like the lines of a checker board. With their red pillars, white walls and tiled roofs, the buildings belonging to government offices, mansions of the nobility and temples gave the city a color and beauty that was extolled in song.

Higashiyama culture

The culture of the middle part of the Muromachi period (1338-1573). The name is taken from the country retreat that the 8th Ashikaga shogun, Yoshimasa, built in the Higashiyama district of Kyoto as a refuge from the ravages of the Onin war (1467-77). There, following the example of Ashikaga Yoshimitsu, the third shogun, he built the Silver Pavilion. His encouragement of the arts gave the period its flourishing culture. Chinese studies (centering on the writings of the Sung period) were undertaken by monks of the Gozan Zen monasteries, while linked verse poetry (*renga*) was promoted by Sogi (1421-1502) and ink painting by Sesshu (1420-1506). The *shoin* style was adapted from Zen temples for the domestic architecture of the warrior class, and the arts of tea ceremony and flower arrangement gained in popularity.

Himeji Castle

One of the best surviving examples of a Japanese castle, located in Himeji in Hyogo prefecture. It was completed in 1610 by the daimyo Ikeda Terumasa (1564-1613), a son-in-law of Ieyasu. It is a castle of the "plain" type, erected on a small hill. The central keep, five stories high on the outside and seven stories high inside, is connected with three smaller keeps. The castle is also known as Shirasagi (Egret) Castle because of the beauty of its white walls.

Horyuji

A temple erected in 607 by Prince Shotoku (574~622), located at Ikaruga near Nara. Destroyed by fire in the middle of the 7th century, it was reconstructed some time after that, and is today the oldest wooden construction in the world. It is strongly influenced by Chinese culture, and in the wooden columns of the inner gate and corridor may be discerned curved shafts like those of Greek Doric columns. The layout of the temple compound, with the main hall (*kondo*) and the five-storied pagoda side by side, is a Japanese innovation, not a Chinese design. Horyuji epitomizes the first great period of Buddhist culture in Japan. Among its treasures are the Shakyamuni triad made by the sculptor Tori Busshi in 623, and the minature Tamamushi shrine, dating back to the late 7th century.

Ikebana

Flower arrangement ranks with the tea ceremony as one of the characteristic arts of Japan. It is also termed the way of flowers (*kado*). During the Muromachi period it was called *rikka* ("standing flowers"). It became valued as an art of appreciation, and was especially popular among the nobility and the Buddhist priests. It spread throughout all classes of society during the Edo period, when various schools proliferated.

Ink Paintings (*Suibokuga*)

Monochrome pictures using only contrastive shades of black ink. They originated during the T'ang dynasty (618-907) in China, and were perfected in the Sung dynasty (960-1279). Ink painting was developed in Japan during the Kamakura and Muromachi periods, under the influence of Sung and Yuan (1271-1368) techniques and styles. It was the painter Sesshu (1420-1506) who brought to perfection a Japanese style of ink painting.

●Himeji Castle

●Horyuji

Kondo

●Ikebana

Nageire

Joruri

Narrative chanting that originated during the Muromachi period and gained in popularity during the Edo period. Towards the end of the 16th century, the *shamisen* was introduced from Okinawa as an accompaniment for voice. The form developed when puppets were introduced to illustrate the chanting. During the Genroku era, the chanter Takemoto Gidayu (1651-1714) perfected the *gidayu-bushi* style, which is still used in the puppet theater today. In Edo, *gidayu* was joined to Kabuki, and further styles of chanting, such as *tokiwazu-bushi* and *kiyomoto-bushi*, came into existence.

Kabuki

A popular form of stage entertainment which was developed during the Edo period. It originated in the performances of dancing and light drama (*kabuki-odori*) enacted by a woman, Okuni, and her group in Kyoto at the beginning of the 17th century. When this "women's Kabuki" was banned in 1629, its place was taken by *wakashu kabuki*, performances by young men, and then after 1652, when that in turn was forbidden, by *yaro kabuki*, "men's kabuki." Kabuki was brought to maturity as a dramatic form with the appearance of excellent scripts and the development of women's roles taken by specialist male actors called *onnagata* or *oyama*.

Kana

Simple syllabic writing systems developed in Japan early in the Heian period for convenience of writing. The term *kana* means "not regular" in contrast to the "real writing" (*mana*) of Chinese characters (*kanji*). *Hiragana* (rounded letters), also known as *sogana* (cursive letters), is a system derived from simplified versions of the cursive style of Chinese characters, and originally was used largely by women. The second of the syllabaries used today is *katakana* (fragmented letters). It dates from the end of the Nara period, when various elements of Chinese characters were employed as phonetic symbols to aid Buddhist priests in reciting texts written in Chinese.

Kanji

Chinese ideographs. The oldest known of these characters are to be found engraved on tortoise shells excavated from the site of the capital of the Yin (Shang) dynasty (c. 1400-1027 B. C.). The Chinese writing system was brought to Japan during the 5th century, and used originally by immigrants from the continent for compiling court records and composing letters to be sent abroad. Gradually characters came to be used more and more widely among the Japanese themselves. They are termed "real writing" (*mana*) in contrast to the

"nonregular" *kana* (see above).

Kasei culture

The designation given to the brilliant culture of the final years of the Tokugawa period, taking its name from the two eras (Bunka and Bunsei) that covered the first three decades of the 19th century. At that time the center of culture shifted to Edo from the Osaka-Kyoto region, and from the rich merchants to the townsmen in general. In content also, the culture became more popular and was widely disseminated. However, the vitality of the culture was weakened by social dislocation and strict shogunal control and the suppressed vigor was diverted to satire. The ideals of understated but perfect taste (*iki*) and connoisseurship (*tsu*) were stressed.

Katsura Detached Palace (*Katsura Rikyu*)

A villa on the banks of the Katsura River west of Kyoto dating from the middle of the 17th century. Built by Prince Hachijo no Miya Toshihito (1579-1629), the younger brother of the Emperor Goyozei, it is a skilful harmonization of buildings and strolling garden, a place of simple beauty.

Kinkaku

The Golden Pavilion. A splendid three storey building that was originally part of the country retreat that the third Muromachi shogun, Ashikaga Yoshimitsu (1358-1408), built at Kitayama in Kyoto in 1397. It is so called because its walls and pillars were gilded. It is a typical example of the Kitayama culture, with a continental Zen temple style incorporated with the traditional *shinden-zukuri* architectural style. The retreat was converted into a Buddhist temple, Rokuonji, after Yoshimitsu's death in 1408. Destroyed by arson in 1950, it was rebuilt in 1955.

Kitagawa Utamaro

(1753-1806) *Ukiyo-e* artist. Trained in the Kano school tradition and in the techniques of print-making. Influenced by the work of Katsukawa Shunsyo (1726-1792) and Torii Kiyonaga (1752-1815), he perfected the print depicting popular beauties. His work is characterized by the half-torso figure, and his expression of individualistic female beauty through concentration on the face and the hands. He brought about a golden age in the representation of women in prints.

Kitayama culture

The culture of the early part of the Muromachi period (1338-1573). It is typified by the Golden Pavilion (*Kinkaku*) built by the third Muromachi shogun, Ashikaga Yoshimitsu, at Kitayama in the northern part of Kyoto. A special feature of the culture is that it encompasses both the Japanese cultures of the warrior class and the court

● **Kabuki**

"Sukeroku"

● **Kinkaku**

● **Kitagawa Utamaro**

"Musume-hidokei"

nobility and the Zen-influenced Chinese culture. The Five Mountains (*Gozan*) literature and monochrome ink painting (*suibokuga*) were developed at this time, and the Noh drama was perfected by Kan'ami (1333-1384) and his son Zeami (1363-1443)

Kojiki

"Record of Ancient Matters," the oldest extant history of Japan. The Emperor Temmu (r. 673-686) initially ordered its compilation, but interruptions occurred and it was the Empress Gemmei (r. 707-715) who saw to the completion of the work, undertaken by Hieda no Are and O no Yasumaro and presented to the Empress in 712. In three sections, the *Kojiki* covers the mythological beginnings of Japan, its legends, and the reigns of its Emperors, using Chinese characters.

Kokugaku (National Learning)

An intellectual tradition of the Edo period that emphasized the importance of the native Japanese tradition especially in thought and literature. In rejecting what was not Japanese, in particular Chinese and Buddhist, National Learning undertook the historical study of old texts to find what was truly Japanese. Kamo Mabuchi (1697-1769) studied the *Manyoshu* and extolled it as the true expression of Japanese feeling. The studies of Motoori Norinaga (1730-1801) of the *Kojiki* and *The Tale of Genji* gave the movement a new classical tradition independent of Chinese or Buddhist influence. An off-shoot of National Learning was the Shinto revival of Hirata Atsutane (1776-1843) and others. Hirata attempted to rouse the national consciousness of the Japanese as Japanese. This in turn influenced the promoters of Imperial restoration, and had an effect on Meiji policy in the first few years of the new government.

Kyoka

(lit. "mad verse") A literary form that was popular during the 18th century. It employs the thirty-one syllable form of the traditional Japanese poem (*waka*) but depends on humor and punning for its effect. It had an appeal that crossed classes, involving both samurai and townsmen. Many of the *kyoka* satire political and social events of their time. One of the best known of the *kyoka* poets was Ota Nampo (1749-1823).

Kyogen

Light comic plays that are performed between separate Noh plays. Thus they are also called *Nohkyogen*. As Noh developed out of the earlier *sarugaku* tradition in the Muromachi period, certain comic roles that had existed in that popular entertainment came to be emphasized. Many *kyogen* have as their subject matter the everyday life of

● **Matsuo Basho**

● **Meiji Restroation**

Emperor Meiji

the common people, and there are also a large number which lampoon the samurai and the Buddhist priests.

Manyoshu

The oldest collection of Japanese poetry, compiled during the Nara period. Divided into twenty sections, it contains about 4,500 *waka* (poems) written by a wide range of people including emperors, nobles, priests and farmers. Famous poets represented include Kakinomoto no Hitomaro, Yamabe no Akahito, Yamanoue no Okura, Otomo no Tabito, Otomo no Yakamochi and Princess Nukada. The name of the compiler is unclear, although the collection has been attributed to Otomo no Yakamochi.

Matsuo Basho

(1644-1694) A *haiku* poet. Originally a retainer of the Todo family of Iga (Mie prefecture), he studied the *haikai* in Kyoto, and moved to Edo on the death of his lord, at which time he gave up his position as a samurai. He continued to devote himself to his poetry, and spent much of his time on journeys, which became the subject matter for original *haiku*. He raised the *haikai* form to unprecedented heights. His collection of verse and anecdotes, *The Narrow Road to the Deep North* is famous.

Meiji Restoration

The restoration of Imperial rule under Emperor Meiji in 1868. The leaders of the restoration movement were largely members of the samurai class from the "outer," non-Tokugawa domains. Though the new government at first contained many who were the ideologues of Shinto restoration, and was supported by the proponents of the *sonno joi* slogan, the emergent leaders showed a willingness to try new ideas, which led to wholesale importation of Western modes, moderation in their ability to resist the demands of ideology in favor of the practical, and an appreciation of traditional ideals.

Momoyama culture

The culture of the Azuchi-Momoyama period (1573-1603). The flamboyant culture with its strong decorative element took form based on the economic strength of the new daimyo class, typified by Nobunaga and Hideyoshi, and of the rich merchants of the Osaka area. In contrast to previous cultural expressions, the art of this time was little influenced by Buddhism. It was rather a secular culture set firmly at the human level. It was heavily influenced by the Western artifacts of the *Namban* culture.

Mono no aware

An aesthetic term denoting sensitivity to the pathos of things as they constantly undergo change. It has become almost synonymous with the artistic and literary ideals of the Heian period. *Aware*, which originally signalled some kind of intense emotion, was used by the Heian nobility to express what was elegant, refined, but ephemeral. The Buddhist teachings of impermanence seem to have influenced the notion.

Murasaki Shikibu

(ca. 978-1016) Author, born into the middle nobility. She began to write *The Tale of Genji* after her husband's death. As a result she became well-known and was summoned to court to attend the Empress, Shoshi, the daughter of Fujiwara no Michinaga and wife of the Emperor Ichijo.

Namban culture

The culture brought by Europeans during the latter half of the 16th century. Much of it was connected directly with Christianity, though it was multifaceted, including astronomy, the calendar, geography, medicine, techniques for movable type printing, oil painting and engraving, food and dress.

Nihon Shoki

"Chronicles of Japan." An historical work completed in 720 compiled at the order of the Emperor by Prince Toneri and O no Yasumaro. It is basically an Imperial history from the mythical age to the reign of the Empress Jito. It was written in classical Chinese and organized according to the Chinese histories. It is, with the *Kojiki*, an important source for the study of early Japanese history.

Noh

One of the classical art forms of Japan. It is a form of drama which developed out of the popular entertainment current since the Heian period, *sarugaku* and *dengaku*, and became perfected as an elegant performing art by the actor and dancer Kan'ami (1333-1384) and his son Zeami (1363-1443) in the 14th and 15th centuries under the patronage of the shogun Ashikaga Yoshimitsu (1358-1408). Five schools now exist: the Kanze, the Hosho, the Kongo, the Kita and the Komparu. Though widely known as Noh, it has officially been called *nohgaku* since the Meiji period.

Oda Nobunaga

(1534-1582) The first of the great reunifiers of Japan after the period of civil war in the 15th and 16th centuries. A daimyo from the province of Owari (the present Aichi prefecture), he defeated the powerful daimyo Imagawa Yoshimoto at the Battle of Okehazama in 1560 and then proceeded to pacify the neighboring province of Mino (Gifu prefecture). In 1568 he installed Ashikaga Yoshiaki as shogun in Kyoto and took control of the government. Yoshiaki took up arms against Nobunaga in 1573, but was defeated and sent into exile, bringing to an effective end the Muromachi shogunate. Nobunaga then subjugated the five provinces of the capital region, and the provinces along the Japan Sea and Pacific Ocean coasts. He built Azuchi Castle in the present Shiga prefecture as his residence. He was assassinated in 1582 by Akechi Mitsuhide at the temple of Honnoji in Kyoto.

Osaka Castle

Erected on the site of the temple, Ishiyama Honganji, by Toyotomi Hideyoshi in 1583. Its construction took three years and the labor of tens of thousands of conscripted workers. After Hideyoshi moved to Fushimi castle near Kyoto, Osaka Castle was put under the control of his young son, Hideyori. It was burned when it fell to the Tokugawa in 1615, but was soon restored by the shogunate. The present keep is a reconstruction dating from 1931.

Otogi-zoshi

Short moral tales written between the 14th and 17th centuries. A large number were composed during the Muromachi period (1338-1573) and were read by townspeople. Tales such as *Monogusa Taro* and *Issun Boshi* have become the basis for modern nursery stories.

Pure Land Buddhism

A general term for those Buddhist doctrines which teach that people can attain rebirth in the Pure Land of a Buddha, Amida (Amitabha) in particular. In Japan they remained for a long time an element of existing sects, but nevertheless dominated Japanese religious thought from the 11th century, and influenced religious art and architecture to a large degree. Pure Land doctrines were brought from China to Japan by various monks during the Heian period and systematized within the Tendai school in particular, from which emerged Genshin (942-1017), who wrote the important treaties on Pure Land faith and practice, *Ojo Yoshu* (Essentials of Rebirth), Honen (1133-1212), who encouraged the single practice of the oral invocation as the only way to salvation and founded the first independent Pure Land sect, the Jodo, and Shinran (1173-1262), who stressed the importance of faith and founded the Jodo Shin sect.

Renga

Linked verse. Consists of alternating stanzas composed by different people based on the two parts of the classic thirty-one syllable poem: the "upper" (*kami no ku*) of three lines and the "lower" (*shimo no ku*) of two lines. Linked verse can continue for fifty or a hundred stanzas. The form originated during the Nara period, and was a type of

●Noh

"Sumidagawa"

●Oda Nobunaga

●Osaka Castle

entertainment among the nobles during the Heian period. Its form was regulated during the Muromachi period, when it spread among the common people and steadily gained in popularity. The poet Sogi (1421-1502) was an acclaimed master of the technique.

Rokumeikan

(lit. "Deer Cry Pavilion") A building constructed in 1883 by the English architect Josiah Conder (1852-1920) in the Hibiya district of Tokyo as a social forum for the upper classes. It reflects the Europeanization of society at the time when Japan was trying to secure the revision of the Unequal Treaties. It was intended to show the world the results of Westernization.

● **Rokumeikan**

Sabi

An aesthetic term denoting pleasure in austere beauty, in what is faded or imperfect. A coarse but often-used tea-bowl of uneven glaze, cracked and mended, may denote it, as may a fallen flower or a moss-covered rock. There is no melancholy engendered, and in this *sabi* contrasts to the *mono no aware* of the Heian period. Basho's *haiku* epitomize the ideal of *sabi*.

Sakoku

The policy of isolation imposed on Japan in the middle of the 17th century by the Tokugawa shogunate. To enforce the ban on Christianity and to ensure shogunal control of overseas trade, Japanese were forbidden to travel abroad and the entry of foreign vessels into Japanese ports was strictly limited. Japanese were forbidden to leave the country in 1635, and in 1639, following the Shimabara Rebellion, in which (Roman Catholic) Christianity had been implicated, Portuguese ships were denied entry to ports. After that, the only foreign trade that was allowed had to be done through the southern port of Nagasaki, and was limited to two countries only, China and Holland.

Sen no Rikyu

(1522-1591) The great tea-master of the Azuchi-Momoyama period. Born in Sakai (near Osaka), the son of a wealthy merchant family, he served both Oda Nobunaga and Toyotomi Hideyoshi, officiating at tea-ceremonies. He brought the tea-ceremony to perfection based on his ideals of simplicity and ordinariness. He was forced to commit suicide after having incurred Hideyoshi's anger.

Senryu

A literary form popular during the latter half of the Edo period. It is composed of seventeen syllables in three lines of five, seven and five. Most *senryu* are a satire of society or a parody of human nature. Since the publication of the immensely popular collection of these verses, *Yanagidaru*, by the poet Karai Senryu (1718-1790) they have come to be called generally by his name.

Sesshu

(1420-1506) A monk-painter during the Muromachi period, the most famous painter of ink paintings (*suibokuga*). He became a monk in the Zen sect at the age of ten, and studied painting. In 1467 he travelled to China and after his return in 1469 perfected a Japanese style of ink painting. Representative of his work are *Landscape of the Four Seasons*, *Autumn and Winter Landscapes*, and *Landscape on a Long Scroll*.

Shell mounds

Mounds made from piles of shells discarded by people of the Stone Age (corresponding to the Jomon period in Japan). Discarded stone and clay utensils, and animal bones have also been excavated from them. They are thus important in terms of archeology. Many have been discovered along the Pacific Coast in particular. The first systematic excavation of a shell mound in Japan was undertaken by the American zoologist Edward Morse (1838-1923) in 1877 at Omori in Tokyo.

Shinden-zukuri

A style of domestic architecture for the nobility perfected in the Heian period. Its central feature was the main hall (*shinden*), to which was connected in the east, west and north annexes (*tainoya*) and pavilions (*tsuridono* and *izumidono*). Each building was joined by passageways (*watadono*). The main hall was fronted by a formal garden of ponds and artificial hills.

Shinran

(1173-1262) A Buddhist priest who lived at the beginning of the Kamakura period (1192-1333). He studied first at the Tendai complex on Mt. Hiei near Kyoto, and then became a follower of the monk Honen, who had left Mt. Hiei to establish a practice of faith in the Buddha Amitabha, based upon the recitation of the *nembutsu* invocation. Exiled to the present Niigata prefecture, Shinran went a step further than his master and founded the Jodo Shin sect, also called the Ikko (Single-minded) sect. He taught that anybody at all can be saved, if they have absolute faith in Amitabha. In particular he advocated that it is particularly the evil man who has the capacity for rebirth. After spreading his teachings widely through the Kanto area, he eventually returned to Kyoto.

Shoin-zukuri

An architectural style used in the construction of the residences of the warrior class during the Muromachi and Azuchi Momoyama periods. Characteristic elements of the style are the *genkan* (entrance hall), the *tokonoma* (alcove), the *chigaidana* (staggered shelving), the *shoin* (built-in desk), and the use of *fusuma* (sliding screens), *shoji* (latticed paper sliding partitions) and *tatami* (matting for floors). It represents an adaption of elements from Zen architecture to the domestic architecture of the warrior class, and is the basis for the modern domestic style.

Shosoin

An ancient storehouse in the compound of Todaiji, a temple in Nara, now under the jurisdiction of the Imperial Household Agency. It is built in the *azekura* style, walls made of interlocking logs. The term *sho-so* was originally applied to the principal storehouses of local authorities and temples, but now it indicates only the storehouse located north-west of the Great Buddha Hall at Todaiji. It is a treasure house of Tempyo culture, containing articles formerly belonging to the Emperor Shomu (8th century), Buddhist implements, and documents.

Tale of Genji (*Genji Monogatari*)

The best-known, as well as one of the earliest examples, of Japanese prose literature, written early in the 11th century by the court lady, Murasaki Shikibu. It is a very long work, of fifty-four chapters, and over a thousand pages in translation. The first part of the work, up till the 41st chapter, paints the colorful "world of the Shining Prince," the life of the court nobility with the hero, Hikaru Genji, as the central figure. The second part of the Tale is more somber, dealing with the dark fate of Kaoru, supposedly Genji's son.

Tea ceremony (*chanoyu*)

The etiquette surrounding meetings for the drinking of tea. It is also called the Way of Tea (*chado*). It is said to have been brought from China in the Nara period, but it was in the Kamakura period that the powdered green tea used in the ceremony was recommended by Buddhist monks to people as medicine. Tea drinking became naturalized during the Muromachi period, and turned into an accomplishment of refined elegance. The procedure was simplified by Murata Juko (1422-1502), and made into a supreme art by Sen no Rikyu (1522-1592).

Tempyo culture

The culture of the Nara period (710-784). It flourished particularly during the Tempyo era (729-749) when the Emperor Shomu was on the throne. It was an aristocratic culture with Buddhism at its center, and heavily influenced by the culture of the Chinese T'ang dynasty. Also apparent is the influence of western Asian and Indian cultures. Typical of the culture are the Buddhist statues of Todaiji in Nara and the treasures of the Shosoin.

Terakoya (Temple school)

Popular schools during the Edo period. Here the children of townsmen and farmers were taught reading, writing and the use of the abacus by teachers who may have been *ronin* (masterless samurai), Buddhist or Shinto priests, or doctors. Texts such as the *Teikin Orai* (a collection of models for letter writing) were used.

Todaiji

A temple built during the Nara period as the foremost of the national temples (*kokubunji*) by the Emperor Shomu. The dedication ceremony of the main image, the Great Buddha, a statue of the Buddha Mahāvairocana, was conducted in 752. The present Great Buddha Hall is a construction of the Edo period, and is only seventy percent of the dimension of the original; nevertheless it is the largest wooden building in the world.

Tokugawa Ieyasu

(1542-1616) The first Tokugawa shogun. Born the eldest son of Matsudaira Hirotada, the lord of Okazaki Castle (in the present Aichi prefecture). As a child he was sent as hostage to the Oda and Imagawa families. Later, in alliance with Nobunaga, he extended his power, and was a party to the unification of Japan under Toyotomi Hideyoshi. He moved to Edo in 1590 when he was granted the Kanto plain as fief. At the Battle of Sekigahara in 1600 he defeated Ishida Mitsunari and his allies. In 1603 he established his shogunate in Edo, but two years later resigned his position in favor of his son Hidetada. Neverthless he continued to wield actual power from his retirement.

●Tokugawa Ieyasu

Toro site

Archeological site which is a good example of Yayoi period (ca. 300 B. C.-300 A. D.) remains. It is located in marshland on the eastern bank of the Abe river in the southern part of the city of Shizuoka. It was discovered in 1943, and excavations were undertaken between 1947 and 1950. Archeologists made rich finds: dwellings, storehouses with raised floors, the remains of paddies, and wooden farming implements such as paddy-clogs (*tageta*), looms, and pestles. It was designated a special historical site in 1952,

Toshogu Shrine (Nikko Shrine)

A Shinto shrine in Nikko, Tochigi prefecture, dedicated to Tokugawa Ieyasu. After Ieyasu died, his remains were interred on Mt. Kuno (Shizuoka prefecture). Hidetada, according to his father's wishes, removed the remains to a mausoleum in Nikko, which was completed in 1617. The third

●Toro site

shogun, Iemitsu, undertook large-scale extensions, which resulted in the shrine as we know it today. The buildings are flamboyantly decorated with ornate carving, gold-leaf and painted designs. The Yomeimon (1636), the main gate, is a good example of the architecture of the period.

Toyotomi Hideyoshi

●Toyotomi Hideyoshi

(1536-1598) A general who brought all Japan under his control in the late 16th century. He was born Kinoshita Tokichiro in the province of Owaki (Aichi prefecture). A retainer of Nobunaga, he was given posts of increasing importance, until he became the lord of Nagahama Castle in Omi (Shiga prefecture) with the name Hashiba Hideyoshi. He heard of Nobunaga's assassination while campaigning in western Japan. Having beaten the assassin, Akechi Mitsuhide, in battle, he assumed the position of successor to Nobunaga. Later he reached a settlement with Tokugawa Ieyasu and by 1590 had united the whole country. In 1585 he had received the title of *Kampaku* (an Imperial designation) and the following year the surname Toyotomi from the Emperor. His cadastral survey and his Sword Hunt (which forced any one not a samurai to turn in his weapons) laid the foundations for a feudal society. His last years were darkened by the failure of his plans to conquer Korea.

Ukiyo-e

(lit. "pictures of the floating world") A form of art depicting the life of the common people very popular during the Edo period. It had its origins in the latter part of the 17th century in the work of Hishikawa Moronobu (d. 1694). Moronobu at first produced ukiyo-e in the form of painting, but soon moved on to the design of woodblock prints and developed the technique of multicolored printing called *nishiki-e*. The golden age of *ukiyo-e* was the first three decades of the 19th century, with the collections depicting popular beauties by Kitagawa Utamaro (1753-1806), the studies of *Kabuki* actors by Toshusai Sharaku (dates unknown) and the landscape prints of Katsushika Hokusai (1760-1849) and Ando Hiroshige (1797-1858).

Wabi

An aesthetic term denoting what is serene and austere. During the turmoil and disruption that marked the Kamakura and Muromachi periods, poverty and simplicity took on a positive value, and were extolled by writers as Kamo no Chomei (*Hojoki*, "An Account of My Hut"). The aesthetic was prized by the tea-masters of the 16th century, and emphasized particularly by Sen no Rikyu (1522-1591). *Wabi* tends to

●Ukiyo-e

"36 Views of Mt. Fuji" by Hokusai

"53 Stations of the Tokaido road" by Hiroshige

denote a way of regarding things, and contrasts to *sabi*, which is closer to an artistic or poetic ideal.

Yamato-e

Japanese style painting, which emerged around the middle of the Heian period. When the embassies to China were terminated, the predominant Chinese styles of painting were replaced by paintings of a Japanese flavor, of soft lines and bright colors, depicting scenery and customs. At first it was used in the decoration of screens (*byobu-e*) but by the end of the Heian period it had developed into the picture scroll (*emakimono*), with works such as the illustrated *Tale of Genji*.

Yogaku

(lit. "Western learning") The general name given Western studies, particularly science, during the Edo period. Things European were first known through the Portuguese and the Spanish traders and missionaries, and later through the Dutch and English merchants, but after the seclusion policy came into effect, all knowledge of the West came through the Dutch at Dejima, and the study of the West was called Dutch Learning (*Rangaku*). The term *Yogaku* came into use in the 19th century when languages other than Dutch came to be studied. European influence was felt in the early period in medicine, firearms, shipbuilding, engraving, etc. and from the 17th century interest centered around medicine, astronomy, geography and military science.

Yokyoku

The chants composed in the Muromachi period, which acted as the script for Noh plays. Zeami (1363-1443) is the best known of the composers of *yokyoku*. During the Edo period it is said some three thousand were composed.

Zen

A sect of Buddhism. It professes not to place weight on the Buddhist scriptures or on ritual, but says that enlightenment can be gained through meditation (*zazen*). The two best known of its schools in Japan are Rinzai transmitted from China by Eisai (1141-1215), and Soto, transmitted by Dogen (1200-1253). Zen teachings spread widely during the Kamakura and Muromachi periods.

Chronology of Japanese

YEAR	200 B.C.	100	1 A.D.	100	200	300	400	500	600	700	800
CENTURY	3rd B.C.	2nd B.C.	1st B.C.	1st A.D.	2nd A.D.	3rd	4th	5th	6th	7th	8th	9

| ERA | JO-MON | YAYOI | | | | | BURIAL MOUND | | | ASUKA | NARA |

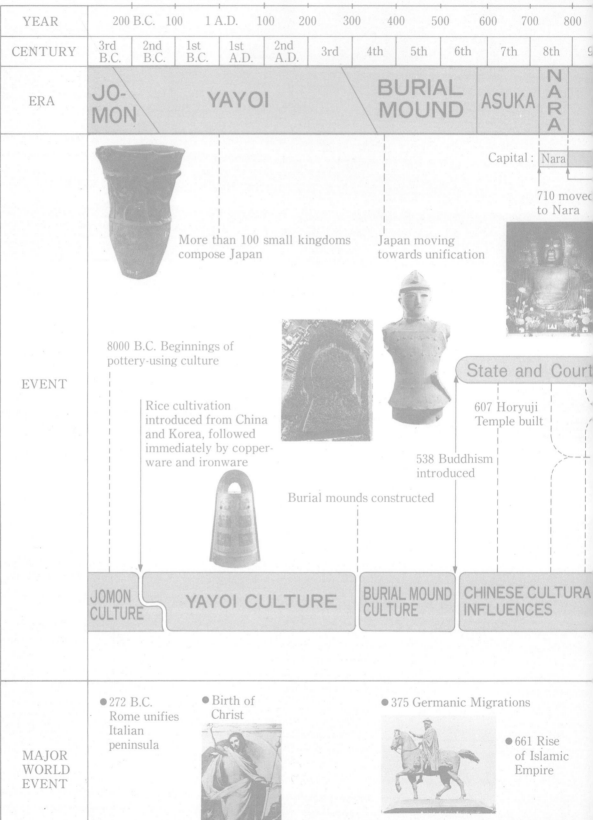

Capital : Nara

710 moved to Nara

More than 100 small kingdoms compose Japan

Japan moving towards unification

EVENT

8000 B.C. Beginnings of pottery-using culture

State and Court

607 Horyuji Temple built

Rice cultivation introduced from China and Korea, followed immediately by copperware and ironware

538 Buddhism introduced

Burial mounds constructed

| JOMON CULTURE | YAYOI CULTURE | BURIAL MOUND CULTURE | CHINESE CULTURA INFLUENCES |

MAJOR WORLD EVENT

● 272 B.C. Rome unifies Italian peninsula

● Birth of Christ

● 375 Germanic Migrations

● 661 Rise of Islamic Empire